D1083655

# Ami and Amile

AMI AND AMILE

translated from the

Old French

by

Samuel Danon

and

Samuel N. Rosenberg

French Literature Publications Company
York, South Carolina
1981

*Nous nous cherchions avant que de nous estre veus, et par des rapports que nous oyions l'un de l'autre, qui faisoient en nostre affection plus d'effort que ne porte la raison des rapports, je croy par quelque ordonnance du ciel: nous nous embrassions par noz noms.*

Montaigne, *Essais I, 28*

# CONTENTS

# Introduction

The story of Ami and Amile is a celebration of perfect friendship.

Its heroes belong to the long line of exemplary pairs—including David and Jonathan, Achilles and Patroclus, Roland and Oliver—that stretches through the centuries of our history and our mythology up to the beginnings of the modern age. Ami and Amile, curiously, are the only ones whose friendship is the very focus of a legend rather than an element, however important, of some larger story.

The ultimate origin of the tale is obscure and no doubt bound to remain so. MacEdward Leach,[1] following Gédéon Huet,[2] traced it essentially to a synthesis of two widespread folktales of peerless fidelity, *The Two Brothers* and *The Faithful Servitor*, with an admixture of other folk themes. Without necessarily rejecting that hypothesis or similar ones, other scholars have stressed as of more immediate significance specifically medieval points of departure. Joseph Bédier,[3] beginning with a pair of tombs in Mortara, one bearing the name Amelius, showed the relation of the legend to the Via Francigena, the route that French pilgrims followed to Rome. Francis Bar,[4] among others, took as the inspiration of the story the well-known friendship of two southern French princes of the early eleventh century.

In all of these cases, however, there is considerable speculation, and little can be generally accepted beyond the notion that, whatever the ultimate source or sources of *Ami and Amile* may have been and whatever the immediate circumstances of its elaboration, the various extant versions of the story probably derive from a chanson de geste originating in the south of France in the eleventh century. Thus, William Calin[5] is willing to acknowledge the presence of folkloric elements in our poem, but, stressing the pointlessness of looking to the preliterary for illumination, concentrates his attention on the far more demonstrable relation between *Ami and Amile* and the epic genre and on an examination of the artistic and moral values of the work itself.[6]

The story occurs in numerous versions. Leach listed thirty-four, stretching from the eleventh century to the seventeenth, and composed not only in continental French and in Latin, but in Anglo-Norman and Middle English, in German, Welsh and several other languages as well. To this inventory, Brian Woledge[7] later added the prose redaction found in twelve French incunabula.

The legend was clearly popular, particularly in its early centuries. The evidence is of course in the plethora of versions just cited. It lies, too, in allusions to Ami and Amile which occur in other works, where they are acknowledged as proverbial friends. Thus, we are told in the thirteenth-century romance *Dolopathos* that the friendship of its two heroes is so deep that it surpasses even that of Ami and Amile; the *Yder,* of the same century, extols the friendship of Yvain and Gauvain in similar terms. Most notable perhaps is the assurance provided by the narrator of the very first extant version of our story: Radulfus Tortarius introduces the tale by asserting that it is as well known among the Saxons as in Gaul.

There is considerable variety in the numerous retellings. Characters change in name and in social status; there are shifts in locale; narrative components undergo modification, substitution, re-arrangement, deletion. But above all, perhaps, matters the extent to which religion plays a role in the story. Leach proposed—and others have generally accepted[8]—the relative presence or absence of a Christian emphasis as a fundamental criterion of classification. To use his terms, the versions of the legend fall into a *romantic* group, in which the ideal friendship and its testing are presented in a basically secular way, and into a *hagiographic* group, in which the virtues of the two friends are rewarded with miracles worked in their behalf and lead them to martyrdom and the exemplification of sanctity.

Of the oldest versions extant, the earliest, dating from about 1090, is clearly of the first type, which we should do well to rename *secular*. It is a Latin verse composition, contained in the Second Epistle of the French monk Radulfus Tortarius and presented as a résumé of a longer, well-known work. The universe of this redaction is wholly non-Christian. Leach, p. xxii, quite rightly calls the poem "pagan and classical" and Francis Bar demonstrates cogently to what length the narrator let himself be inspired by such ancient sources as Cicero's *De Amicitia.*

The next version to survive, from the first half of the twelfth century, is the anonymous Latin *Vita Sanctorum Amicii et Amelii (Life of Saints Amicus and Amelius)*,[9] which is apparently the immediate, or at least the never very remote, source of all the subsequent hagiographic tales.

Somewhat later, there is the Anglo-Norman *Amis e Amilun,* written about 1200. As for the English version of the legend, its oldest manuscript dates from about 1330, but the poem itself appears to have been composed considerably earlier and may well be at least as old as the Latin *Vita.*[10] Both the Anglo-Norman and the English works, though hardly so resolutely non-religious as the version of Radulfus, belong to the secular group.

Of the two basic treatments of the legend, there seems little ground for doubt that the quite spare, secular handling is close to the original story, now lost, while the hagiographic represents a considerable elaboration of the basic tale, together with a displacement of its emphasis.

Our own poem, no doubt composed around 1200, was classed as secular by Leach and has usually been seen as such by later scholars as well; these include Peter Dembowski, who is responsible for its recent critical edition.[11] It is nevertheless obvious that the work is more than passingly expressive of a Christian spirit. Similarly, it is ordinarily considered to be a chanson de geste, yet there is much about it that is clearly not epic. *Ami and Amile* is in truth a work that draws on several sources of inspiration and brings together components of various genres.

To begin to appreciate its complexity, we may simply attempt a simultaneous view of its narrative and that of Radulfus' epistle.

Ami and Amile are born on the same day in two different parts of France. They are both taken to Rome, where they are baptized at the same time by the pope, who presents them with identical drinking cups; they are then returned to their respective homes. [Radulfus makes no mention of this episode.] Hearing that they resemble each other like identical twins, the two boys are eager to meet. At the age of fifteen, each sets out in quest of the other; they eventually come together and swear eternal friendship. [This mutual search does not occur in Radulfus.]

The two youths go together to Paris, where they enter the service of Charlemagne as knights. [In Radulfus, they go—separately—to the court of the king of Poitiers, and it is only there that they meet and become friends; there is no more mention of Charlemagne than there was of the pope.] The companions achieve such success as warriors that Hardret, the emperor's seneschal, becomes envious and plots their death. The scheme fails, but Hardret avoids disclosure by offering his niece Lubias to one of the friends. Ami accepts and leaves Paris for Blaye, where he will live with his new wife. From the start, however, it is clear that Lubias is a malevolent woman and that the marriage is doomed. [No part of this sequence is found in Radulfus.]

Back in Paris, Charlemagne's daughter Belissant offers her love to Amile. Rejected, she seduces him one night through a sly concealment of her identity. Hardret happens to witness the scene and proceeds to denounce the couple. The emperor plans a judicial combat between the steward and Amile. The situation is critical, since Amile is, after all, guilty and thus cannot hope to defend himself successfully. He sets out to seek the advice of

Ami, who, warned of danger in a dream, is already on the road to Paris. [In Radulfus, we learn only now that Ami, newly married, and to a woman unrelated to the villain, is no longer at the royal court; there is no dream-warning, and Amile must travel all the way to Ami's home.] The friends agree to profit by their extraordinary resemblance and change places. While Amile is in Blaye posing as his friend (but abstaining from conjugal relations with the latter's wife), Ami, truly innocent of fornication with Belissant, enters the combat and triumphs, killing Hardret. [In the course of the battle, which proportionally receives far greater attention in the Latin text than in the French, the latter's numerous invocations of the Christian deity are matched in Radulfus by Classical allusions, including one to Mars. Radulfus does, however, introduce a sword which had once belonged to Roland and, before him, to Charlemagne.] Charlemagne, pleased with the outcome, offers his daughter to the triumphant knight, who, compelled by circumstances and despite an angel's warning that he faces the punishment of leprosy [this divine intervention does not occur in Radulfus], falsely betrothes her as if he were indeed Amile; with Belissant he then sets out for Blaye on the way to the dower city of Riviers. At Blaye, the couples are sorted out; Amile and Belissant, now married and happy, leave for Riviers.

Ami is stricken with leprosy. Instead of giving him wifely support, Lubias publicizes Ami's illness, obtains a decree of separation, and relegates him to a pauper's hovel. Their young son Girard tries to help his father, but is soon stopped by Lubias, who does, however, consent when two faithful serfs propose to care for Ami and take him to his godfather, the pope in Rome. Upon the pope's death, Ami, ever weaker, seeks a final haven with his brothers in Clermont, but is turned away. With the two serfs, he finds his way to Riviers, and Amile, who has long wondered about the fate of his companion, recognizes the disfigured leper by his goblet and gladly offers him a home. [In Radulfus, Ami is driven out at the first sign of leprosy and goes directly to Amile, who needs no mark by which to recognize him.]

One night an angel announces that the dying Ami can be cured, if he is washed with the blood of his friend's children. [Radulfus has this remedy proposed by doctors.] Amile, though

horrified, proceeds to sacrifice his children, and the cure is ef-
fected. No less miraculously [for Radulfus, marvelously], the
beheaded children are then restored to life. [Radulfus' version
ends here, with Ami going away well. Near the beginning of his
narrative, he mentioned, however, that the friends now lie buried
in "well-known tombs."]

The two companions go to Blaye, where Ami establishes his
son and decides to pardon Lubias, and then journey to the Holy
Land to seek forgiveness of their sins. They both die on the way
back home, and their tomb becomes a landmark for travelers.

Alongside the spareness of Radulfus' primitive text, the
French chanson de geste presents a rich and finely detailed story,
which brings together in a unique and coherent blend elements of
several major medieval narrative genres. The presence of the
*hagiographic* is indisputable. Beyond the simple birth-to-death
completeness of the lives which it recounts—a trait more typical
of hagiography than of any other vernacular narrative type, but
which in itself is hardly consequential—the chanson reveals much
of the explicit Christianity of the *Vita* and much of its exemplifi-
cative character. The divine presence is undeniable as a constant
reference and support, and the miracles of the *Vita*, which by the
very nature of the genre we need hardly demonstrate, suffuse the
chanson de geste as well. From the divinely ordained birth of the
two identical heroes, underscored by their papal baptism,
through angelic predictions first of leprosy and then of recovery,
to the miraculous blood-cure itself and the still more miraculous
resurrection of the children, the tale unfolds in the same atmosphere of Christian wonder that marks the *Vita* inherently.

Closely associated with that atmosphere, and with the
hagiographic redaction, is the theme of a somewhat supernatural-
ly guided quest, wholly alien to Radulfus and presented in a
geographic framework borrowed from the realities of medieval
pilgrimage. Not only do the youthful heroes set out simultane-
ously in search of each other and achieve their remarkable encounter partly through the help of a holy pilgrim; their reunion

after Hardret's denunciation of Amile, too, is hastened by a warning of danger that Ami has received in a dream, and the leprous Ami succeeds in his final quest for Amile thanks once again to the intervention of a man of God. But we must question the degree to which Christianity is significant in the French poem and doubt whether the object of testing and exemplification in the poem is indeed the same saintliness that we necessarily find in the Latin work.

If we bear in mind the secular spirit of the early story, such as it emerges in Radulfus' account (or in the English or Anglo-Norman versions), it is highly probable that the composition of the chanson de geste was influenced by the *Vita,* with which moreover it shares other, non-religious features, particularly the Carolingian setting. But however notable the Christianity of the chanson may be—and Calin, for one, has attempted to place it at the very heart of the work—the poem cannot be read as a tale of saints and martyrs without distortion of the text.[12]

The second half of the action stems from Ami's willingness to take the false and bigamous oath of betrothal in full knowledge of its sinfulness and of the dread disease that will ensue. It is hard to grant, however, that the burden of the whole period following the onset of leprosy is the gradual expiation of Ami's sin, if there is nowhere in the text any sign that Ami ever regrets having committed it or, for whatever reason, wishes that he had not. None of the atonement that we should expect in a hagiographic tale is to be discerned in the chanson. Its very absence is in fact a striking proof that the poem is above all concerned with ideal, and secular, friendship: everything, even obedience to God's law, must yield to the advancement of that good.

It seems an exaggeration to speak, as Calin does, p. 111, of Ami's wanderings as a "quest for salvation." The text of the poem much more readily supports the view that the goal of Ami's search is an opportunity to live out the rest of his leprous life in a way as dignified and as physically and psychologically comfortable as may be—if at all possible, in the beneficent presence of friendship. No less distant from the saintly is the death of the two heroes. Calin, again, speaks of that end, p. 111, as "their final abnegation," as "the highest manifestation of Christian virtue." "*Contemptus mundi,*" he states, "opens the gates to the Heavenly City and eternal love." But it is hard to see the companions' death, unexpected during their journey home from Jerusalem and certainly not sought for, as abnegation; it is no less hard, a short while before, to detect *contemptus mundi* in their decision—itself never a question, besides—not to remain penitents at the Holy Sepulchre, but to return home instead. In the *Vita*, a final military campaign allows the two heroes to do battle for their Lord and end their lives as religious martyrs; the divine embrace is then tightened by a miraculous joining of their separate tombs. Such events are absent from the chanson de geste, and to speak nonetheless of martyrdom, of "following Christ (*imitatio Dei*) in his Crucifixion" (p. 98), of "becom[ing] Christ" (p. 112), is to distort the sense of the French text.

There is a hagiographic strain, then, in *Ami and Amile* and, more precisely, there is clear evidence that the poem was influenced by a hagiographic version of the legend, no doubt the *Vita* we still possess. But the making of saints is far from being the central concern of our work, and its considerable Christian component can be more fairly regarded as a very powerful enhancement of the ideal friendship it portrays. The poet well understood that, to impress his audience with the exemplary character of the heroes' supreme fidelity to each other, the two friends must be made generally exemplary, too—and in the terms of their own society. They are thus warriors of rare prowess, husbands and fathers of singular devotion, and—within the limits imposed by the material of the story—strikingly pious and worthy Christians. The miracles performed in their behalf work further to raise their stature, and so serve the purpose of extolling friendship. The divine restoration of the children, in particular, serves not merely to prevent the heroes from being irremediably tainted by the atrocity of their murder, but to justify that sacrifice as convincingly as possible for a Christian audience.[13]

However important the religious component of the chanson de geste may be, it remains of secondary interest, a well-developed graft. For traditional Christian values are in conflict with the very material of the story (and even the *Vita* cannot entirely succeed in resolving the conflict[14]). Belissant is a sensual temptress whose advances to Amile are the first cause of all the companions' woes—yet she is presented sympathetically from the start, and not simply later when she gives proof of her nobility and love.  Hardret's denunciation to the emperor is, strictly speaking, an act of truth and loyalty; his willingness to defend himself in judicial combat can only stem from the belief that, as a messenger of the truth, he will be supported by God— yet from the beginning the steward is clearly presented as thoroughly evil, and not simply later when he proclaims his allegiance to Satan.  Amile does not hesitate to lie to Charle- magne in response to Hardret's accusation and, with Ami, does not scruple to stage a sham battle whose deceit would implicate God himself—yet the heroes are never made the object of any reproach for such behavior.  No less a sin than the murder of innocent children is committed, yet it is not allowed to dim the admiration with which the friends are always regarded.  Clearly an ethos not traditionally Christian is at work in the very core of the poem, even if, through the concept of a higher and a lower justice, an accommodation may be achieved.[15]

In short, *Ami and Amile* shares certain important features— not all religious, for there is the Carolingian setting as well—with a specific work of hagiography, the *Vita,* which it does not share with the other early versions of the legend.  Then, it shows analogues to the themes of pilgrimage and quest and salvation which are typical of the hagiographic genre, and certainly in- corporates the basic hagiographic element of the miracle.  Final- ly, we may see as a parallel to the function of hagiography the edifying portrayal, from birth to death, of a type of morally ideal heroes and the celebration of a type of exemplary behavior.

The *epic* component of the chanson is appreciably more evident and less subject to dispute.  It is in fact so great that, whatever may be said of the influence of other genres and the ultimate significance of the work, no one has persuasively ques- tioned the use of the term *chanson de geste* as the most fitting conventional label.  There is the form, first of all, which is typical of the Old French epic genre.  The work is intended for declamation by a first-person narrator before an audience addressed in the second person.  "Now hear me, noble lords. . . Today you will hear about two goods friends," the poem begins, and the presence of the author—or of his surrogate, the *jongleur*—will be manifested sporadically throughout the recitation in an effort not, mainly, to explain the action or express a point of view, but to encourage a lively interest on the part of the listeners—"There was nothing he needed that he did not have right away, save good health, which he longed for above all. But that, I can tell you, was on its way, too" (126)—and to reinforce the articulation of the narrative structure—"Here we'll take leave of Amile the brave and tell of his friend Ami, who was in Blaye in his big house" (48).

The poem unfolds in sections of unequal length, known as *laisses,* each of which contains verses of identical meter—lines of ten syllables—all held together by a single final assonance; the end of each *laisse* is signaled, however, by a verse that is both shorter than the others and unassonanced. The following pair of consecutive *laisses* will make the form clear:

> 4  Eight verses, assonance in *-e-:*
> Li cuens Amis est venus en Nevers.
> A Verdelai se randi vrais confés,
> Puis remonta el bon destrier qu'iert frés,
> Passa avant li gentiz prouz vaslés,
> Droit en Borgoingne s'en vait li ber apers.
> Parmi Mongieu fu moult grans li yvers,
> Passe Mortiers et Chomin et Chastel.
> > Ez le voz en Pavie.

> 5  Eleven verses, assonance in nasal *-o-:*
> A Traves vint Amiles de Clermont
> Et va querrant dant Ami le baron.
> Mont Chevrol puie tant que il vint en som,
> Tant que il vint a Borc c'on dist au pont.
> La se harberge chiés un oste felon.
> Icelle nuit i jut li gentiz hom
> Et au matin s'en vint en Pré Noiron.
> Iluec demande de son bon compaingnon,
> Mais il ne treuve escuier ne garson
> Ne clerc ne lay qui l'en die raison.
> > Tornéz s'en est en Puille.

Another compositional trait of the epic genre is the occur-

rence of *laisses similaires,* or groups of *laisses* in which the event
of the first is repeated in the second (and third, as the case may
be), often with some factual difference or some variation or further development in the outcome, or in which the event of the
first is actually followed by a similar event in the next *laisse.*
This parallelistic device usually serves to ensure the impact of a
particularly dramatic moment. Perhaps the most striking occur-
rence of the procedure is the one in *laisses* 151 and 152, which
even finds an echo in 153:

151
. . .When he [Amile] saw that he was all alone in the palace and
could act without being seen, he took his sword and a golden
bowl and went straight to the room where the two boys were lying
side by side.

He found them asleep in each other's arms; their beauty had no
match even as far as Duurstede. He gave them a long and tender
glance. His distress was so great that he fell to the floor in a faint,
and with him fell the sword and the golden bowl.

When he came to himself, the good knight sighed: "Wretch that
I am, what can I do?"

152
Count Amile was distraught and bewildered. He dropped to the
floor in a faint, and with him dropped the bowl and the bare steel
sword.

When he recovered his senses, he said: "Amile, wretch that you
are, born to behead your own children! Yet what does it matter,
if my deed will restore a man who is scorned by the world and regarded as dead? Now he will be brought back to life!"

153
Count Amile faltered for a moment. He stepped slowly up to
the children; he found them asleep and gazed at them for some
time. . . .

The *laisses similaires* are a product of the public, oral per-
formance for which the Old French chansons de geste were conceived. It is in all likelihood to the same source that we may

attribute a second, very important, formal characteristic by which *Ami and Amile* reveals that it belongs to the epic genre: the widespread use of a formulaic diction.[16] This refers, *grosso modo*, to fixed or closely related phrases, metrically uniform, sometimes composed by a given poet but often adopted from others, which are repeated frequently, in various combinations or contexts, to express action or sentiment, description or characterization. With little or no particularizing force and with a clear metric identity, they were a broadly useful tool for facilitating the recitation of usually illiterate *jongleurs*. Thus, a reference to any admirable character may be followed, in the six-syllable segment of the epic line, by the laudatory formula *qui moult* (or *tant*) *fait a prisier* 'who merits (so) much esteem'; or various departures from town may be repeatedly announced by the full line *Parmi la porte issent* (or *issi*) *de la cité* 'Through the gate they go out (he went out) of the city.' A departure by one of our poem's heroes is often expressed in the four-syllable part of the verse by *Va s'en Amis* (or *Amiles*) 'Off goes A.,' which is usually followed by some formulaic epithet of six syllables such as *li preus et li cortois* 'the valiant and courteous' or *li cortois et li fiers* 'the courteous and proud.' Such formulae are one of the hallmarks of the genre.

When we move from the form of *Ami and Amile* to its substance, we find numerous other elements that are characteristic of Old French epic poetry. Friendship itself, though not alien to chivalric romance, is thematic in epic, where it is a natural attribute of the feudal world at arms, of which this genre is the poetic expression. It stems from the oath of loyalty that unites vassal and lord, but more particularly from the shared experience which unites one vassal with another in the service of a common lord. The term "companionage," sometimes used to denote the first of these relations, is usually applied to the second.[17] In either case, it is the institutional basis of knightly friendship and ensures the presence of that affection in epic poetry. The chansons de geste offer numerous examples of pairs of friends, the most celebrated being Roland and Oliver. Occasionally the bond between the two men is reflected in similarity of names, such as Gerin and Gerier or Ivoire and Ivon. It is this tradition which accounts for the names Ami ('friend') and Amile.

The epic world is one of warfare and violence and is pre-eminently male. Women and amatory concerns are largely absent from it, and even the few striking female characters who do occur—Guiborc, for example, in the *Song of William*—are of peripheral interest. *Ami and Amile* proves to be no exception; indeed, one may even speak of a certain anti-feminism in the poem. Lubias is unmitigatedly evil, a sensual, cruel, and mendacious woman, as incapable of love for her son Girard as for her husband Ami, and as intent upon destroying the bond between father and son as that between the two friends. Belissant, for all the virtues she has and for all the approbation with which she is presented, nonetheless makes her appearance in the poem as an avatar of the temptress Eve and, in that role, sets the stage for the heroes' misfortunes. If she develops into a very model of wifely and motherly devotion, it is perhaps mainly so that she may serve as the work's most persuasive internal celebrant of the all-overriding friendship of her husband and Ami. The attitude toward women typical of the genre and inherent in our story is manifested in specific words of the heroes themselves. No passage is more succinctly expressive of the view of woman as biological instrument than the one in which Ami, replying to Amile's courteous request for news of his wife, says with equal courteousness and probably with no conscious shift of focus: "This news: I have a son by her, finer than any in France" (31). A short while later, Ami warns his companion away from the possible advances of Belissant, "for once a woman has a man, she makes him forget father and mother, cousins and brothers and all those closest to him" (34). And as well-mannered as the two men are, neither does Ami hesitate to counsel slapping Lubias in the face if she should say anything arrogant or untrue (60), nor does Amile shrink from acting upon that advice (62).

One of the salient features of the genre is the presence of a traitor who plays a prominent role within the ranks of the good and within the main action of the story. Just as the *Song of Roland* has its Ganelon, *Ami and Amile* has its Hardret, seneschal and confidant to the emperor, a figure of innate villainy whose unleashing of dire forces is less a product of some objective cause than of opportunity. It happens—and this is certainly one of the

strengths of the poem—that Hardret has quite clear motivation
for wickedness: envy of the two companions and fear of being
displaced in the royal court's esteem by their superior prowess
and general appeal; but we are given to understand that beneath
the surface of such explicitation lies an implicit will to evil
whose existence is independent of events. Hardret, in fact, is a
recurrent traitor, for we find him again in *Garin le Lorrain* and
*Gaydon,* among other chansons de geste. But the villain is rarely
alone, and it is very much part of the feudal picture that his
whole family should share his malevolence. Thus, Lubias needs
no special reason to behave as she does; as Hardret's niece, she is
implicated in evil by definition. And it is only normal that when
Hardret attempts to direct his godson Aulory toward a career
of doing ill, the latter should reassure him: "Have no fear, godfather. . .it's been more than three years since I last felt any urge
to do good" (83). Underlying this convention of blood-de-
termined moral sameness is, to be sure, the historical reality of
clan cohesion, which demanded family responsibility for the
conduct of any individual and drew the entire kindred group
into any act of vengeance or defense.[18] Amile acknowledges
this institutional solidarity, and not only the treachery common
to all of Hardret's kin, when, going to sleep for a while on his
journey toward Ami, he nevertheless remains armed, for "he was
in fear of his enemy Hardret and the thousand men of his clan
who wanted to kill him" (52).[19]

No less striking a characteristic common to our poem and a
great number of other chansons de geste, perhaps more striking,
is the Carolingian setting. The world of Charlemagne is the epic
world *par excellence,* and it is in that supremely heroic context
that Ami and Amile prove the strength and the indissolubility
of their perfect friendship. The Carolingian setting, then, friendship, a martial life, the distinctly marginal and second-class role
of women, the traitor, blood-ties—these are all notions typically
associated with Old French epic in general and expressed in
significant measure in *Ami and Amile* as well.

Finally—and this is not unrelated to the presence of Charlemagne—there is the element we may call epic truth, the historic
core of the work by which the poetic fabulation is linked to
events of the past still present, albeit through tales, in the mind
of the audience. It is this truth which defines epic above all else.

Objectively, it is quite clear to us that *Ami and Amile* is a work of fiction,[20] but that modern perception must not prevent us from seeing that it has that special historical veracity which underlies all medieval epic. In the words of Hans Robert Jauss,[21] p. 65, "for the audience of the chanson de geste, historicity does not have the modern sense of factual truthfulness; in its view, rather, any event or any experience is historical which asks to be believed [and] the authors of the chansons de geste always asserted the truth of their epic tales. . .even when they wove legend inextricably into history" (my translation). Indeed, we need only look at the first laisse of *Ami and Amile* to find such an affirmation of truth: "It is no mere tale that I have just made up myself, but the truth," says the poet, who then calls upon "many people—monks and clerks and priests—[to] testify to that" and reinforces his assertion by referring to a real tomb—ostensibly that of the heroes—in a real geographic setting. As early a commentator as the medieval poet Jean Bodel identified such historical truth as an essential mark of epic poetry, distinguishing it from romance. From a modern point of view, we may say that the fundamental fiction of the chansons de geste, whether their creators realized it or not, is the claim that they are not fictitious. In support of this claim, the poet of *Ami and Amile* is careful to place the extensive travels of his heroes in a toponymic framework which is almost entirely real. While it is possible that Riviers is an invention and while Joincherres may be as well, most of the place-names in the narrative, and even some of the churches alluded to, are well grounded in reality. A concern for realism and credibility is typical of Old French epic, particularly during the period of our poem, and is expressed in *Ami and Amile* not only geographically, but also in other ways. In addition to the realistic depiction of such major facets of the story as leprosy and the judicial combat, there is evidence of that concern, as Calin points out, p. 72, in "details relating to the state of serfdom in medieval France, problems involving travel by sea, famine and subsequent inflation in Rome and Berry, aspects of urban politics (Lubias stirring up the bourgeoisie and commons against the bishop, to have Ami banished)."

If it is indisputable that *Ami and Amile* is most appropriate-
ly regarded as a chanson de geste, it is no less true that certain
aspects of it are more readily associated with other Old French
narrative genres. We have already seen the link with hagiography.
In another respect, the poem seems more consonant with *courtly
romance,* for it relates a personal story of knighthood rather than
a public one. As Jauss maintains, p. 72, "the epic action of the
hero in the chanson de geste remains subordinate to the larger
destiny of the Christian and national community, and is thus
integrated into an order of events which are supra-personal and
objective" (my translation).   This is an echo of Erich Auerbach:[22] "in the chanson de geste. . .a knight who sets off has an
office and a place in a politico-historical context. It is doubtless
simplified and distorted in the manner of legend, but it is main-
tained insofar as the characters who take part in the action have
a function in the real world—for instance, the defense of
Charles' realm against the infidels, their conquest and conversion, and so forth.   Such are the political and historical purposes
served by the feudal ethos, the warriors' ethos which the knights
profess."

It is hard to recognize Ami and Amile in such statements.
The chanson de geste named for them is not concerned with any
public issue, any political or historical or religious cause which
would subsume their story. The poem is focused, rather, on their
lives and their relationship, and while the two companions certainly do battle against the enemies of Charlemagne and France,
it can scarcely be said that the activity constitutes a center
of interest in the narrative. Not only in the space allotted
to it, but also in its political or historical scope, the common
cause—defeat first of the Bretons and then of Gundbald of Lorraine—is remarkably insignificant. The most urgent cause and the
most obvious adversary for an epic of the late twelfth century
are never even mentioned, although there is ample opportunity
for their appearance: twice, voyages are made to Jerusalem (in
laisses 6 and 176), yet nowhere do we find even an allusion to
the Crusades or the Saracens. At a time of intense awareness of
the struggle between the Christian and Moslem worlds, the com-
poser of a chanson de geste had to make a deliberate effort to
avoid all reference to an issue of such import.

How much closer the career of the two companions appears

to Auerbach's summary of Arthurian knighthood, where there is "no political or historical task [and] the feudal ethos serves no political function; it serves no practical reality at all; it has become absolute. It no longer has any purpose but that of self-realization" (pp. 116-117). If, for the series of adventures which the hero of romance consciously seeks in order to "prove his mettle," we substitute the successive trials by which Ami and Amile uncover and prove the strength of their friendship, the parallel becomes even more plain: the chivalric experience is "raised to the status of a fated and graduated test of election; it becomes the basis of a doctrine of personal perfection through a development dictated by fate" (p. 118).

Through a series of tests, the life of the saint, too, leads to the attainment of a personal ideal and an exemplary perfection, and we may say that hagiography and courtly romance, in a somewhat curious alliance, work together as an underpinning for our epic companions. Two quite different genres reach into the chanson de geste to explain the strangely non-epic intensity with which it idealizes a virtue that, while not peculiar to epic, is most closely identified with it. And at the same time that the hagiographic component of *Ami and Amile* serves to underscore the perfection of the two heroes, its very presence reveals too that that perfection is not a Christian one. Similarly, the very parallel with romance, in which the ideal attainment necessarily and deeply involves the love of woman, shows the friends' exemplary achievement to be non-courtly.

In this light, the Carolingian setting of the poem, which, as we have seen, does not provide the work with an overriding public importance, reveals its true purpose: to enhance the nobility of the two friends by placing them against a background of the highest heroic worth. The earlier versions of the legend make it clear that Charlemagne represents a secondary elaboration, a product, as Bar points out, p. 61, of the "centralizing tendency of the [epic] poets, or, better, the power of attraction of a well-known epic cycle" (my translation). The setting of our poem is thus, in part, an employment of what had become a convention of the epic genre. More important, however, that particular conventional setting—there were other choices possible, after all, and they were occasionally used—gives to the two heroes a measure of external valorization that no other could provide. The legendary greatness of Charlemagne, associated with Ami and Amile, serves to ennoble their tale and add luster to their ideal friendship; it is the most prestigious setting that the conventions of the epic genre made available.

Like the Christian element we saw earlier, the Carolingian presence in the poem has an essentially utilitarian function: they both serve the purpose of extolling exemplary friendship. And Charlemagne here has no more centrality or politico-historical substance than King Arthur has in romance. As in the courtly tales, all interest is concentrated on the heroes themselves; their story is detached from any notion of religious or secular mission.

In its episodic structure, the poem presents a series of convergences and divergences of the heroes' lives which reflects in spatial terms the arduous progress of friendship. Their meetings are demonstrations of their affection; their separations, tests; and the cumulative movement is toward an unbreakable and everlasting union.

The poem falls quite clearly into five divisions:

1.  Birth and baptism; mutual quest and encounter (laisses 1-13).

2.  Life at Charlemagne's court—
    a.  demonstration of chivalric valor, causing Hardret's enmity; Ami's marriage, departure, return, and new departure (laisses 14-34);
    b.  Belissant's seduction of Amile, Hardret's betrayal, plan for judicial combat (laisses 35-47);
    c.  reunion of Ami and Amile and exchange of identities (laisses 48-60).

3.  The judicial combat—
    a.  Amile at Blaye (laisses 61-67);
    b.  the combat (laisses 68-84);
    c.  the false betrothal (laisses 85-92);
    d.  reunion of Ami and Amile in Blaye and new separation (laisses 93-102).

4. Ami's leprosy and wandering—
   a. Ami at Blaye (laisses 103-123);
   b. wandering (laisses 124-135);
   c. arrival at Riviers and reunion with Amile (laisses 136-141).

5. Ami's new life—
   a. the cure (laisses 142-167);
   b. voyage to Blaye and Jerusalem; return and death together (laisses 168-177).

Each division is marked toward its end by a significant re-union of the two heroes; these major points of convergence, in fact, occur at regular intervals of approximately forty laisses (11-12, 54-55, 96-97, 139-140, 177) and thereby imprint the theme of union in friendship upon the very rhythm of the poem. In terms of narrative time,[23] the first three meetings are all followed rather quickly by separations, for the testing of the knights' devotion is not yet complete. Once it is clear that their friendship is perfect, however, no further divergence is possible; when, after the cure, Ami suggests that he would leave Riviers to visit his family (laisse 168), Amile does not hesitate to undertake the voyage with him. The luminous sacrifice that Ami made for Amile, accepting the living death of leprosy, has now been matched by the sacrificial infanticide of Amile, and both extraordinary acts of love—one through miraculous healing and the other through a miraculous resuscitation—have now received divine sanction; the friends can never again be separated. Even death then becomes, not a parting, but a final consecration of their bond, for they die together, share one tomb, and, the poet tells us, will be celebrated as a pair "till the end of time."

It is assumed here that the reader has a sufficient familiarity with the French Middle Ages to understand in general the social and political context in which the action of *Ami and Amile* takes place. In many ways, of course, the poem speaks for itself. In addition to a few particulars of the age which have been mentioned in the preceding pages, however, there are two major historical elements of the poem which call for special comment.

The first is the institution of the *judicial combat;* the second, the disease of *leprosy.*

Trial by battle[24] is one of the numerous physical ordeals by which medieval justice attempted to distinguish truth from falsehood and innocence from guilt in both civil and criminal litigation.   Of ancient origin, it is neither peculiar to western Europe nor peculiarly Christian in nature, although most characteristic of medieval judicial procedure.   It represents an early attempt to overcome the barbarous violence of right-through-might.   The judicial combat can use violence in the service of impartial justice in any society that believes in the power of truth, through one deity or another, to assert itself against whatever odds.   In Christian Europe, truth was of course seen as an attribute of God, and trial by battle was validated by the belief that divine intervention would guide the physical struggle to a just conclusion; with God's sure help, truth and innocence would prevail.   The practice was widespread in the adjudication of cases showing a lack of conclusive natural evidence.   Since the combat began with a solemn oath by each contestant affirming the justice of his cause, defeat was not merely a loss of the suit or a proof of guilt, but a conviction of perjury as well and to be punished as such.

The representation of the *judicium Dei* that we find in *Ami and Amile* is a quite accurate one.   Hardret, as plaintiff, makes his accusation before the king and presents his gage, the usual glove; Amile accepts the challenge (43-45).   The two contenders then obtain hostages, who will be held responsible, on pain of death in this case, for ensuring that their bailees appear, ready for combat, at the appointed time (45-46).   On the day of the duel, the poem omits the occasional presence of a priest and the saying of Mass,[25] but properly shows the king presiding, attended by his court, and the adversaries each swearing upon relics that he alone is in the right and that the other is lying (73).   While the ceremony is not presented in its most complete form, the text does include the interesting detail of the command that, on pain of bodily harm, all spectators shall maintain the impartiality of silence during the fight (75).   Again, it is normal that the contest should be halted at nightfall (82).   At the conclusion of the combat, the defeated antagonist must be punished for his perjury; since Hardret is not merely vanquished, but dead, the punishment takes the form of desecration of his body (87).

If trial by battle was an ordeal that human justice imposed on occasion, leprosy[26] was one that the Middle Ages lived with constantly and believed to be imposed by God. The affliction was far more widespread then than now, and the inability of diagnosticians to distinguish from its symptoms those of various other maladies of the skin gave it an extraordinary prominence in medieval life. It was a terrifying scourge, leading only slowly and through a repulsive deterioration of the body to inevitable death, and it was all the more horrible as, considered contagious, it entailed a ruthless banishment of the sufferer from any normal social existence. Endemic since ancient times, it had long been seen as the most fearsome of diseases and had over many centuries acquired a mythic status in which its physical reality was but the outward manifestation of a moral state: leprosy was no less a disease of the soul than of the body.

While the Church often took the position that leprosy was, paradoxically, a mark of divine favor, a special grace and certain road to salvation, even a form of identification with Jesus, the prevailing view was that the disease was a Heaven-sent consequence of sin, both a physical sign of spiritual corruption and a punishment for it. Both attitudes are revealed in the contradictions that marked society's treatment of lepers. While edict upon edict purposed to thrust them out of the community of the healthy and into leprosaria or isolated hovels, the circulation of lepers in towns and on roads was in fact a common phenomenon. If they were the objects of loathing and vilification, they were, too, the recipients of compassion and charity. The religious ceremonies which initiated their sequestration were usually a veritable office for the dead, expressing the principle that lepers did not belong to the ranks of the living; yet the Church, in general, did not hold that the disease justified the dissolution of marriage. Leprosy was regarded as necessarily fatal, but curative efforts were not unknown. Nowhere do we find a consistent policy or consistent practice in medieval behavior toward the afflicted.

This complex reality is well represented in *Ami and Amile*, as it is in a number of other literary works of the Middle Ages, such as Hartmann von Aue's *Der arme Heinrich* and the

Provençal *Jaufré.* Ami is clearly stricken as a result of sin and divine displeasure, but the ultimate restoration of his health is no less clearly an act of special grace. The entire episode of his removal from Blaye, with its depiction of varying attitudes toward him, from Lubias' cruel contempt to the touching charity of Girard, is reflective of historical truth, not the least interesting parts of which are the uncertainty about the proper comportment of a healthy wife and the considerable role of political power. Sequestration is followed by wandering and more evidence of widely divergent approaches to the leper; his mendicancy is a fact of the times, and the grisly progress of his disease is described in all the familiar terms of medieval symptomatology. Even the final healing is no invention of the poet, but the expression of a traditional belief, no doubt of Biblical origin, that the guilt of leprosy could be washed away by the blood of innocent children.

As the most terrible ordeal that the medieval imagination could conceive, leprosy provides *Ami and Amile* with the supreme means of testing the heroes' friendship. Ami willingly accepts the condition for the sake of Amile, and Amile, to restore him to life, commits himself to a cure that no other man would countenance.

Samuel N. Rosenberg

## Translators' Note

To render our Old French poem accessible to contemporary readers of English, we did not hesitate to opt for prose as the appropriate medium. A verse pattern modeled on the original would have led to grave distortions of meaning and a stilted quaintness totally at variance with the tone of the Old French; any choice of verse more modern or more natively English would have produced a sense of distance from the original text even more striking than prose and, in any case, quite pointless. The language of the poem is simple, rather popular than bookish, and undistinguished. We have tried to imitate that register with a kind of minimally Latinate, present-day English as natural and plain as the wholly alien material of the story would permit. While poetic effects inherent in verse have obviously been sacrificed, we have incorporated others, such as epic formulae and certain declamatory rhythms, that would be both consonant with the original work and wholly acceptable to modern readers. And the translation is as literal as possible.

The first ever done into English, it is based principally on the excellent critical edition recently prepared by Peter F. Dembowski.

Brief notes have been added to elucidate a variety of matters in the text, including a few realia of the medieval world, place-names,[27] and the narrative itself.

Notes to Introduction

[1]Introduction to *Amis and Amiloun* (London, 1937).

[2]"Ami et Amile: les origines de la légende," *Moyen Age* 30 (1919), 162-186.

[3]*Les Légendes épiques,* 2nd ed., rev. (Paris, 1917), II, 178-254.

[4]*Les Epîtres latines de Raoul le Tourtier: Etude de sources. La Légende d'Ami et Amile* (Paris, 1937), pp. 27-108.

[5]*The Epic Quest: Studies in Four Old French Chansons de Geste* (Baltimore, 1966), pp. 57-117.

[6]For a general survey of the question of origins and themes, see J. A. Asher, *Amis et Amiles: An Exploratory Survey* (Auckland University College, Bulletin No. 39, Modern Language Series No. 1, 1952).

[7]"*Ami et Amile:* les versions en prose française," *Romania* 65 (1939), 433-456.

[8]E.g., Kathryn Hume, "Structure and Perspective: Romance and Hagiographic Features in the Amicus and Amelius Story," *Journal of English and Germanic Philology* 69 (1970), 89-107.

[9]Published in the Introduction to Eugen Kölbing, ed., *Amis and Amiloun* (Heilbronn, 1884), pp. xcvi-cx.

[10]See Leach, p. xx.

[11]*Ami et Amile,* Classiques français du moyen âge, No. 97 (Paris: Champion, 1969). The only previous edition was by Konrad Hofmann (Erlangen, 1852; 2nd ed., rev., 1882). Both are based on the sole surviving manuscript of the work: Paris, Bibliothèque Nationale, fonds français, MS 860, apparently dating from the second half of the thirteenth century.

[12]For the most extreme reading of this kind, see Thomas E. Vesce, "Reflections on the Epic Quality of *Ami et Amile: Chanson de Geste*," *Medieval Studies* 35 (1973), 129-145, and my response to it in *Olifant* 3 (1976), 221-224.

[13]Francis Bar, p. 98, points out that we have here an indication, among others, of the relatively primitive nature of Radulfus' account. He maintains that it is unlikely, if the homicide had been divinely sanctioned in the original tale, that that feature could have disappeared from any later versions; since it does not occur in Radulfus, it must be a subsequent addition to the story.

[14]See Hume, p. 94.

[15]See Ojars Kratins, p. 351 in "The Middle English *Amis and Amiloun: Chivalric Romance or Secular Hagiography?*" *PMLA* 81 (1966), 347-354, on this problem in the Middle English version. Calin, pp. 83-91, offers a very perceptive analysis and justification of the French poet's attitude toward the behavior in question, but carefully, and no doubt wisely, avoids any outright attempt to explain it in Christian terms. For an instructive discussion of the development, in twelfth-century moral philosophy, of the doctrine of intention as a moral gauge of conduct, see Colin Morris, *The Discovery of the Individual, 1050-1200* (New York, 1972), pp. 73-75.

[16]Formulaic diction in the Old French epic has been a subject of considerable study and debate in recent years. For a survey of the issue and some bibliographic guidance, see C. W. Aspland, *A Syntactical Study of Epic Formulas and Formulaic Expressions Containing the -ant Forms in Twelfth Century French Verse* (St. Lucia: University of Queensland Press, 1970), pp. 1-38, and the review by P. F. Dembowski in *Romance Philology* 28 (1975), 665-668; Joseph J. Duggan, *The Song of Roland: Formulaic Style and Poetic Craft,* Publications of the Center for Medieval and Renaissance Studies, UCLA, VI (Berkeley, Los Angeles, London: University of California Press, 1973) and P. F. Dembowski's review in *Romance Philology* 31 (1978), 663-669.

[17]For a rather extensive discussion of companionage and its historical development, see Leach, pp. lxv-lxxi.

[18]See Marc Bloch, *Feudal Society,* trans. L. A. Manyon (Chicago, 1961), pp. 123-130.

[19]It is significant that the concept of the clan's psychological or moral sameness which stems from its socio-political cohesion does not extend to the family of Ami. When the leper seeks refuge with his brothers, they mock him and send him on his way. This is of the highest importance, for it underscores the poem's insistence on the supreme value of friendship. Once past the opening laisses, we never hear of Amile's family again; now Ami's family, too, must prove unworthy and disappear so that we may most unmistakably perceive the two companions as forming, through their friendship, a "family" of their own. One need hardly add, in this regard, that they have always had the physical (and moral) attributes of absolutely identical twins. As Calin, p. 76, reminds us, moreover, the very word *amis* signifies, in the medieval world, not only friends or allies, but blood relatives as well. (See, too, the passage in Bloch referred to in the previous note.)

[20]As briefly mentioned earlier, Francis Bar, pp. 65-74, following the proposal of J. Koch, *Ueber Jourdain de Blaivies* (diss. Königsberg, 1875), advances the theory that the remarkable friendship of Guillaume Taillefer II, count of Angoulême (d. 1028), and Guillaume V, duke of Aquitaine (d. 1030), served as the immediate, historically accurate, inspiration for the earlier chanson de geste from which our poem probably derives. He is careful not to claim that friendship—and events in the careers of the two princes which are more than slightly reminiscent of elements of *Ami and Amile*—as the ultimate or even principal source of the epic, but speaks of a certain incorporation of the historical material into the material of the legend. Leach, although rejecting the friendship of the two Williams as a specific model (p. xxxiv), does grant that the poet of the eleventh-century chanson de geste "perhaps had in mind an actual friendship, and so wrote his poem in honour of actual persons" (p. lxxxviii).

[21]"Chanson de geste et roman courtois au XIIe siècle," in *Chanson de Geste und höfischer Roman: Heidelberger Kolloquium, 1961* (Heidelberg, 1963), pp. 61-77.

[22]*Mimesis: The Representation of Reality in Western Literature,* trans. W. Trask (Garden City, 1957), p. 116.

[23]Narrative time is the flow of time experienced by the auditor or reader of the poem, the amount of time it actually takes to hear or read the text. It is far more significant in the auditor/reader's perception of the relative importance and of the coherence of events in the story than the temporal movement which the story attributes to those events and to the lives of the protagonists. This is particularly true in *Ami and Amile*, where, on

the one hand, the technique of the *laisses similaires* often halts or reverses the natural flow of time and where, on the other hand, no lengthy passage of time is indicated by any device more convincing than the simple statement that a given period has elapsed. There is thus something unreal, something quite external to the auditor/reader's experience of the story, about the declaration in laisse 12 that the young heroes' search for each other has lasted as many as seven years or about Ami's statement in laisse 33 that he has been in Paris, far from Lubias and his son, for, again, seven years; what matters for the time-consciousness of the auditor or reader is that Ami's present stay in the city began only minutes before in laisse 31.

[24]What follows is based principally on the detailed account in Leach, pp. lxxix-lxxxiv, and on Henry Charles Lea, *The Duel and the Oath* (1866; rpt. Philadelphia: University of Pennsylvania Press, 1974), edited and with an introduction by Edward Peters.

[25]Opposition to the judicial combat on the part of the Church began building during the eleventh century, and papal decrees of 1198 and 1215 specifically condemned the practice (although not to immediate effect). It is no doubt for that reason that the Church is represented in our text only by holy relics.

[26]What follows is based principally on Saul Nathaniel Brody, *The Disease of the Soul: Leprosy in Medieval Literature* (Ithaca, 1974) and on Paul Rémy, "La lèpre, thème littéraire au moyen âge," *Moyen Age* 52 (1946), 195-242.

[27]Our main sources for toponymic identification were K. Körner, "Über die Ortsangaben in Amis und Amiles," *Zeitschrift für französische Sprache und Literatur* 23 (1908), 195-205; Bédier, *op. cit.*, II, 178-254; and the review of Dembowski's edition of the poem by Philippe Ménard in *Romance Philology* 26 (1972), 462-466.

# AMI AND AMILE

Translated by

Samuel Danon and Samuel N. Rosenberg

# 1

Now hear me, noble lords, and God grant you pardon. The valor I sing must never be forgot. It is no mere tale I have just made up myself, but the truth, as true as a sermon, and many people—monks and clerks and priests—will testify to that. The pilgrims who go to Santiago de Compostela certainly know whether it is true or not.

Today you will hear about two good friends, Ami and Amile, conceived as a holy voice had foretold and then both born on the very same day. The good barons now lie buried at Mortara. Today you will hear the tale of these two friends and how at Paris they served great Charles in great companionship.

# 2

Even before Amile and Ami were born, an angel sent by God had told of their great friendship and fidelity. They were conceived on the same night and were baptized on the same day, and their godfather, Ysoret, was none other than the pope in Rome. He was generous and kind, and gave them gold and silver in abundance and the finest silks from across the sea. And for each he had a goblet made, marvelous pieces cast in the same mold; no man alive could see any difference in size.

Amile was then taken home to Berry, Ami to Auvergne. They did not see each other until fifteen years had gone by and they had just been dubbed knights. Talk of each other, though, they often heard, for they were alike in every way. They had the same eyes, the same nose and mouth; they walked alike and rode alike, bore their arms alike, so that neither could be said to be the finer young man.  God had worked a miracle in making them.

## 3

Count Ami, in new armor, left his land one day, left in Auvergne father and mother, young sisters and four brothers.  He came to Bourges to seek count Amile; there he asked for news of the knight who would be his companion, but he learned nothing.

## 4

Count Ami came to Nevers.  At the abbey of Vézelay he made his confession; then, mounting his fresh horse, the noble young man continued on his way, now into Burgundy.  He crossed the Alps at Monjeu in the dead of winter and passed through Mortara and Chomin and Chastel.  He paused at Pavia.

## 5

Meanwhile, Amile came from Clermont in search of lord Ami. He went through Traves, climbed Mount Chevrol to the very top, and came at last to Borgo near the bridge in Rome.  The handsome young man spent the night at a tawdry inn and in the morning went to Nero's Gardens. There he sought news of the knight who would be his good companion, but he found no boy or squire, no clerk or layman who could give him any word. He went on then to Apulia.

6

Count Ami, in the meantime, crossed the Garigliano, passed through Apulia and Calabria, rode on to Sicily. Along the coast stood no castle, no city, town or inn, where he did not go in search of his friend. Count Amile traveled toward the East and his friend to Jerusalem, then back to Gascony.

7

Hear me, noble lords! Let's return to count Amile. In the saddle of his high-spirited charger, he was riding on steadily, careful only not to tire the good horse, when he came upon a pilgrim. He was old and as white as hawthorn in spring. He had sought God by land and by sea; there was no place in the world, no place in Christendom, no good church of God, which he had not visited and where he had not disciplined his body and mortified his flesh.

As soon as the count saw him, he cried out: "God save you, brother pilgrim! In the many lands where you have been, tell me, by the faith you owe the Lord, have you seen a man who looks like me?" The palmer said: "Let me think. Yes," he said, "now I remember! At Easter I was in Siena—that town without a peer in all of Christendom—when a Frenchman came up to me, dressed and armed just like you. Ami was his name; he was from Clermont and had been seeking Amile for a good two years. He had to go back to France, but he could not stop talking about him."

When the count heard that, he began to weep. He leaned toward the palmer, who was standing beside him, and three times kissed his nose and chin. "Brother pilgrim, Heaven be yours! The friend you speak of I have never seen, but I have heard that we are alike in the way we walk and ride and bear our arms. Just for having heard you speak of him, I'll give you this niello ring. If you ever wish to sell it, wherever you may be, it will bring at least a silver mark. I beg you, in the name of our crucified Lord, to tell him, if in any town you should happen on him again, that this poor wretch wants to talk with him. I have never seen Ami, but have been longing for his friendship." The palmer said: "Don't be troubled; simply stay on this road as it turns toward Apulia."

8

Off went Amile, noble knight that he was, and the palmer continued on his way. Not long afterward, he came upon lord Ami beside a cliff at the edge of a heath. The pilgrim recognized him as soon as he saw him, and very politely addressed him: "In the name of God, sir, what a wonder this is! Yesterday morning you were in such distress when you spoke to me of your companion... Turn back along this straight road. So help me God, I am not very courteous; I should really have led you on the way."

### 9

Noble Ami was valiant and quick, and realized at once that it was his valorous friend the palmer had met. From his alms-bag he pulled out two besants and gave them without further ado to the old man. Then, with a kick of his silver spurs, he rode off after the count.

### 10

Off went Ami, spurring his charger, galloping ahead; then he moved into a steady trot. On his way, he came across a boy who was guarding his herds—pigs and sheep up and down the road. As soon as the count saw him, he called out: "Friend, good brother, God protect you! Have you seen a worthy man go by, who looks like me in every way?"

"Not I, sir," the shepherd answered; "so help me God, you're the only person I've seen today. Don't you remember, sir, the rich present you gave to the pilgrim on the bridge? Just take this road back.-- So help me God, you must be mad! He should have led you on the way!"

### 11

So stunning were these words that count Ami wanted to dismount and rest awhile as soon as he could. He soon came to a stream; when he had crossed it, he removed the saddle and let his horse lie down; when both rider and mount were rested, he saddled the animal and rode off again. Before he had gone half a league, he saw straight ahead a field that was covered with flowers as in summertime.  And there he saw, astride his steed in the middle of the field, count Amile!

He had never seen him, yet knew him instantly by his fine armor and all else he had heard described.  With a kick of his golden spurs, he rushed toward him, and Amile, who had seen him from afar, recognized him in turn.  He raced forward, and the two met in such a tight embrace, so mighty was their kiss and so tenderly did they clasp each other, that they almost fainted dead away; their stirrups snapped and they fell together to the ground.  Only now would they speak.

12

The two counts were sitting in the field.  No man in God's creation would not have been moved to see how they embraced and rejoiced in each other.  "In the name of God, sir," said count Ami, "it pains me to think how long I looked for you.  For seven whole years, I never stopped wandering around in search of you."

"Dearest friend," answered Amile, "I, too, for seven years, I searched for you.  Now God has granted us to be here together... Let's go off to court in Paris.  The king is at war; if he is willing to retain us, I will be your liege and vassal, for I see you are a fine and worthy man."

### 13

The two counts were sitting on the grass. They made a pledge of lasting friendship. Then they saddled their mounts and, hands clasping new-made swords, went riding off through towns and cities. They made no pause or stop till they reached Paris.

There the king was ready for war; he gladly let the two barons enter his service, for he saw they were fine and worthy men.

### 14

On the very day they came to Charles' court, the Bretons raised their war-cry. The French gathered in the livestock and raised the bridge. Then Charles' men made ready: with hauberks on and round helmets strapped down, swords fast-buckled on the left and lion-blazoned shields hanging from their necks, they leapt onto their Aragonese chargers and took up the royal standards. The gates opened, the drawbridge was lowered, and they rode out in strength and numbers. Till they reached the lookout, they made no stop.

But there! There you could have seen a wicked battle—helmet after helmet smashed and endless bucklers split, and everywhere men tottering dead to the ground. The two companions fought bravely and well: they captured two counts, Berart and Nevelon, and sent them off to prison in Paris.

Charles was glad and his daughter, the beautiful Belissant, was delighted—but faithless Hardret, as you will now hear, set about to betray and kill the two companions.

## 15

That night they all rested. The next day at dawn, our noble emperor arose and dressed and went to mass and matins in the chapel. His offering made, he went out to walk in the garden. With him was guileful Hardret, who in his sly way began: "True Emperor, God has helped you, and you hold your enemies in chains. You have the two in prison who were the leaders of this attack. Now let me tell you, dear true Emperor: release all your soldiers, count Ami and lord Amile, and give each a hundred-weight of pennies and a mule for his comfort. If they wish not to remain nearby, then have them lodged at a distance. That is what I wanted to tell you."

## 16

Our emperor understood the traitor. "Hardret," he said, "you have a wicked heart to speak so harshly of the two companions. You ought to have said we should give them gold crowns. Go away now, leave me; I don't care for your guile."

## 17

Our emperor was upright and noble. Hardret was base and sly. He was quite ready to give the right answer: "Just Emperor, I was merely testing you. Do treat the new knights well! All my wealth is at your disposal—everything I have, every penny. Let Ami and Amile, counts and warriors both, hold four castles in fee, or whatever rich counties you like." The king said: "Now you are speaking as you should, and what I hear is reasonable and right." Then they went up into the vast palace.

As soon as the proud counts Amile and Ami saw the king, they rose to greet him; then they sat down again on the marble floor. In front of them sat that traitor Hardret. "Lords," he said, "you can count me your friend: I have been of great help to you with the king. He has just now pledged to me that he will give each of you four castles in fee or a rich city." The counts said: "Can that really be true? May God in His justice see how sincere you are with us and how well we know it."

## 18

Our emperor was noble and brave. Out of righteous anger, he had gone to war with Gundbald of Lorraine a good twelve, even fifteen, years before, and no peace or truce or other agreement was yet in sight. One morning, then, Hardret, that accursed traitor, rose, saddled his horse and rode off, galloping through the countryside without a stop till he reached Nivelles. Under the olive tree, he dismounted, then went up the steps to the great stone hall and made his way through the crowd of knights.

As soon as Gunbald saw him, he began: "Sir Hardret, God save you, whose safe-conduct brings you to our city?" The traitor answered: "Yours, good lord. I am hated by the king and queen, and two hirelings of theirs, Ami and his companion Amile, are envious of me. For your sake and mine, have them cut down and killed, and I'll give you one thousand pounds."

Gundbald said: "Thank you, good sir!" He went ahead and pledged his word that the counts would be cut down and killed. Then the loathsome traitor took his leave. With a wicked "God be with you," Gundbald sent him on his way.

19

Hardret went off, taking the leave that Gundbald was so ready and willing to grant. He ran down the marble steps, found his mount below and jumped into the saddle. He dashed through the countryside, past castles and towns and through cities; not once did he stop until he reached Paris. He dismounted at his lodgings, where he stayed through the night until daybreak.

In the morning, when he saw the light of day, he arose and went to church to hear mass. When the good counts Ami and Amile saw him, they asked: "Lord Hardret, where have you been?" "By God, lords, to tell the truth, I went to Saint Lambert's to pray for you. I've done much and have gone to great pains for your sake." The counts said: "We are well aware of that."

Meanwhile, Gundbald was gathering his men, sending summonses throughout his lands until he had a good four thousand under arms. They set out right away and never stopped once until they reached Paris.

There, on the other side of the river, they rode straight into a thick little wood planted with yews and laburnum and olive trees. There the traitors set up their camp and stayed through the night until daybreak. A messenger, God curse him, was sent up to the city. He hurried straight to the palace and up the steps into the great hall. He saw Hardret and went over to him.

Hardret whispered greeting into his ear: "Friend, good brother, where is Gundbald encamped?" "In God's name, sir, he is in the little wood, together with a thousand well-armed knights."

"In God's name, sir, he has acted bravely. Now I will send out a company of knights, together with the two counts whom Gundbald is to slay. Tell him, brother, to be sure they don't escape." The messenger said: "I won't fail to tell him." Then the messenger, God curse him, turned back and left Paris without a moment's pause, and that's the plain truth.

## 20

Hardret behaved like a traitor and scoundrel. He came to the counts, and this is the tale he told them: "Lords," he said, "I have just learned that Gundbald is on his way with a great company of men; he is to be here before the hour of prime. If you now showed your prowess, our emperor Charles would be very glad." Many men heard these words and rushed off to seize their arms. Hauberks on and helmets fastened, they rode out, led by Hardret, that traitor, that scoundrel. God curse him!

## 21

The knights rode out of the town, gleaming hauberks on their back and pointed green helmets on their head, making no stop till they reached the lookout. They were led by Hardret, that forsworn traitor. Jesus Christ curse him!

## 22

Straight to the lookout went the knights. They were attacked right away, first by one troop, then by another. Then you could have seen a mighty battle—shield after shield smashed and endless lances broken, and everywhere men falling down dead. The two good companions fought very well; they captured a pair of well-known counts and sent them off to Paris. Charles, our emperor of France, was greatly pleased and his heart was overjoyed. The two friends then went back to the battle, which was thick and fierce.

Hardret, too, had come out onto the field. Off to a side, under an olive tree, he saw two noble knights lying dead, slain with swords of steel. Hardret went up to them and cut off their heads and hung them on his saddle: he would go back to court and boast of his prowess to all the most famous barons and would appear even prouder and braver. Please God he not last another month! He came to the Seine and waded across, that scoundrel, so full of himself and all his proud clan.

## 23

Oh, that treacherous Hardret has strange intentions, with those two heads hanging from his gilded saddle! He made his way straight back to Paris.

Before all the people who were there, he cried out in his ringing voice: "What say you, my lord and true Emperor? Your enemies have retreated and are fleeing so fast that they have already passed Joincherres. As for your special defenders, what a pity they ever joined the fight! They are lying dead at the bottom of the valley."

The king heard these words and turned pale. Belissant heard Hardret and fell down in a faint.

## 24

Charles' daughter was roused from her faint. God! how she mourns the good baron Amile! "Ah, gentle friend, what a loyal and worthy man you were! God never grant my soul a day's rest, if it was not a traitor that led you into battle! I am sure it was that villain Hardret, bent on destroying my father."

## 25

The emperor heard these sharp words and hurried over to Belissant. "My dear daughter, stop accusing Hardret; he is a good knight. He did very well in the battle; he killed two valiant knights."

Hardret said: "Now I hear a proper statement! Now I hear goodwill and friendship! Count Ami was a very fine knight, and so was lord Amile, who bore your standard. I am very sorry their lives were so short. But if it please you, sir, grant me the charges that the two counts had before the battle." And the king said: "Gladly and with pleasure; I could not give them to a better man."

Why did that hateful hypocrite accept them? A day would come when he would lose his head for such an act! For the two counts indeed came back, bringing with them a pair of good swift horses and two worthy barons whom their knightly valor had let them capture.

## 26

Charles' daughter saw the counts arriving and rushed out to greet them. "Lords," she said, "you are brave and bold. You are on friendly terms with Hardret; I swear to you, though, that that foul son of a cowardly clan hates you, and hates you bitterly; you can be sure of that. It won't be long before you are enemies of his." The counts said: "We know it for certain and plainly admit it."

## 27

The emperor, when he saw the counts return, was overcome with joy. Our noble king went up to Hardret and addressed him angrily: "Coward," he said, "what villainy did you think up?! Covetous traitor, you who claimed that the counts were slain, how could you have such a shameful thought? I am going to accuse you of treason so loudly that all my men will hear it, all the men of France, those courageous knights."

Amile, hearing this, broke in: "Just Emperor, do not suspect him. I saw Hardret break through the great throng and smash his lance and push back his foes."

Hardret heard and did not hesitate. Quickly, he stepped up to the counts and whispered: "Lords, keep my great shame a secret. I'll give you a thousand ounces of gold, as well as beautiful blond Lubias. I'll make one of you rich and powerful."

## 28

Hardret said: "Sire, rightful Emperor, grant Amile a rich reward:
Lubias, my brother's daughter, who is lovelier than a siren or
fairy." The king said: "Bless the day that she was born! Take
her, sir; her father was a rich and powerful man." Amile said:
"Sire, rightful Emperor, let my companion have her; he is a better fighter and strikes better with the edge of his sword." Then
Ami said: "By my father's soul, if she's given to me, I'll take her.
Not by me will she be rejected!" Hardret's kinsmen, hearing
that, were overjoyed.

They rode out of town through the iron gate and galloped
ahead through the countryside, never pulling in their reins until
they reached Blaye. There they found Lubias under a pine tree
in the meadow. Wasting no time, they led her to the church,
and there the gentle knight wed her. All those worthy mothers'
sons made a great feast for Ami and his bride.

## 29

Count Ami wed Lubias. A greater wedding feast than theirs
you'll never see. She, though, right from the start—what a scold
and a shrew! If ever she can, she'll betray him and rob him of
the friendship of Amile. But the good Lord above, I tell you,
won't let her, for count Ami is a man of great sense.

## 30

One night the warrior was in bed with his wife. After they had enjoyed and delighted each other, the wicked woman began: "My lord," she said, "I am very surprised at count Amile, your dear companion. He is very sorry that he didn't take me for a wife; he has sent me four messengers to tell me that gladly and with pleasure he would still have me and love me."

"Lady," said Ami, "you are saying a wicked and sinful thing of the best man who has ever lived. By the apostle we call pope in Rome, nothing could stop me, even at the cost of my limbs, from going to him tomorrow at dawn. And I will take with me four hundred knights who have pledged me their loyalty."

31

It was May. The meadowlark and all the birds were singing, and the sun was bright. Ami set out with a thousand lancers and rode without pause until he came to France.

There he found lord Amile. Ami embraced him, and Amile asked: "Dear friend, what news of your wife?" And Ami said: "This news: I have a son by her, finer than any in France. He will serve you with shield and lance if you ever need him."

32

The comrades-in-arms, then, were reunited in France. Whatever Amile had, he shared with Ami. Our emperor Charles, who loved them both, would have made a fine present to Amile, but he was hoping for the fief of Valsecrée, where baron Godefroy had his men assembled.

But our emperor Charles had a daughter, Belissant, who was beautiful and honored by all. She had fallen in love with Amile, and Charles would gladly have given his consent. You may be sure she would have been delighted! If only Amile had been willing, the match would have taken place in a trice and maidenhead been lost.

### 33

It was April, the time of Easter, when the song of the birds is bright and gay. Count Ami went walking in a garden; he heard the sound of the birds and their warbling, and he remembered the land he was from and his wife and his little son. He was weeping softly, when his companion appeared. Amile at once asked him: "What is wrong, my gentle friend?"

"Dear friend, it's a simple matter. Seven whole years have passed and gone by since last I saw my wife and child. Do I dare admit it? I think that in order to see them I would gladly leave as soon as the sun next rises."

### 34

"Dear friend," said good Amile, "it is right and just that you should go to see them, because a man is duty-bound to honor his wife. But one thing I hope and pray: dear friend, never forget me."

Count Ami said: "There is no need to say that. You have all my loyalty and may count on me as long as I live. But one thing I want to tell you: don't become a companion to Hardret. He would soon bewitch you and betray you and bring you to such shame and grief that things could never again be set right. As for Charles' daughter, don't be tempted by her love; stay away from her arms and let her body be. For once a woman has a man, she makes him forget father and mother, cousins and brothers and all those closest to him. Always remember the vixen under the tree and how she stretches up after all the ripening fruit; she never tastes it, since she can't reach it."

Count Amile said: "Just as you wish. But in God's name I beg you again, dear friend, that you never forget me."

While the two counts were so absorbed in speaking, evening had come on and the sun had almost set. They went to the king to ask his leave, and our emperor was quick to grant it. Ami and his men straddled their fresh mounts and took the main gate out of the city. Count Amile escorted them a good long league and then turned back, but not before the two companions had clasped each other in a close embrace. They parted in tears.

## 35

Off rode Ami, gracious and brave; Amile turned back to Paris.

The good baron went walking one day in a garden; close behind him followed that hypocrite, Hardret. "Ah, Amile, cousin, fine knight! Charles loves me well: I am his counselor and I am the one who pays those who fight for him. It's the man I choose who reaps a rich reward. We can be companions, you and I, sir, if you agree."

The count said: "That is unthinkable. I already have a companion and lifelong friend, to whom I pledged only the other day that, under God's whole heaven, I would never have another." Then wily Hardret answered: "Sir, I would like at least to be on good terms with you and help you become more familiar with this land." And the count said: "By my head, that I accept!"

That was a foolish thing the count did. I can tell you a time came not much later when events took a serious turn, and it almost cost him his head.

## 36

Count Amile was noble and good. If only he could have freed himself of Hardret!

Charles' daughter, fair Belissant, came all in tears to speak to the count. She addressed him in plain words.

## 37

"Good lord Amile," said the noble young woman, "the other day in my room, dressed only in my shift, I offered you the service of my love. You knew quite well how to decline my offer. Yet you have responded very differently to Hardret, who is basehearted and cruel and treacherous. He could never do any harm with his sword, but with his guile he has taken the lives of a thousand men or more." The count said: "Let it not trouble you, fair friend; so help me God, it pains my heart, but there is nothing I can do about it."

## 38

Count Amile was coming down from the tower; the daughter of
king Charles came up to him. Over an ermine-lined robe she was
wearing a long cloak of vermilion silk. She saw the count and
said: "My lord, I love only you. Call me to your bed one night,
and my whole body will be yours."

The count said: "My lady, this is surely a mistake. You are
sought by the mighty king of Aragon and by Girard of Spoleto,
the son of Otto, who heads a host of more than a thousand
comrades-in-arms. You would not take them for all the gold in
the world—how can you want me? I have not a single spur, no
town or city, no castle or tower; I have never had my own
hearth or house. No, I would not do it for all the gold in the
world. But I will be your liege man, madam, and serve you
freely and at any cost, for this indeed I am bound to do."

## 39

Count Amile and the daughter of king Charles parted then in
some displeasure and each went his way along the marble stairs.
That night, count Amile slept in the great hall in a wide bed
adorned with gems and bordered in gold. In front of the count,
a tall candelabrum was burning, and from her room the young
girl could see him.

"Ah, God," she said, "dear heavenly Father! Has there
ever been another man of such proud knighthood, of such
prowess, of such nobility, who has not deigned to love me or
even look at me? But by Jesus, our heavenly Father, I will not
be stopped from doing what I want to do: no woman has ever
been so determined as I! I will go to his bed tonight. I will

lie down among the pelts of marten on his bed. And no matter
to me if all the world sees me or if my father has me beaten for
it daily! Amile's beauty is all that counts."

40

The lady, then, was heartsore to be so spurned by count Amile.
At midnight all alone she arose; she woke no servant or chambermaid to help her. She threw a fine cloak of purple silk over her
shoulders, put out the light and in black darkness found her
way to the bedside of the count. She lifted a corner of the precious marten cover and, slipping in, lay down beside the count.

The count awakened, all confused, and said: "Who are you,
full of passion, coming into my bed at such an hour? If you're
someone's wife and truly married, or the daughter of Charles
who rules France, I beg you, my sweet friend, by God the son of
Mary, let me be and go back. But if you're a servant-girl or
chambermaid, you've done yourself a good turn: stay here with
me, let's enjoy ourselves, and tomorrow you'll have a hundred
sols in your purse."

She was delighted by what she heard. She drew closer to
the count; she did not say a word, but stayed perfectly quiet.
The count felt her body to be slender and delicate, and could
not help being aroused by her love. Her little breasts touched
his chest with their nipples hard as stones, and the noble baron
took his first plunge.

It was just before the second that, from the next room
where he lay awake, Hardret heard them. Oh, God! what woe
would come of that!

## 41

The gentle lady appealed to the count: "Lord," she said, "listen to me for a moment. You spurned me, but with a shrewd play I've now moved in and taken you. Give me your love from now on; be my friend and be my lover." At this, the count became very angry. "Lady," he said, "you have indeed beguiled me and undercut my loyalty to the king. If he learns of this, I will surely lose my head."

From the next room where he lay awake, Hardret heard. In his loud voice, he began to shout: "By God, Amile, you've made bold progress! You really have something to boast of, I see! My lady is a rich reward for you to carry off from court. But you're caught in the act, and if I but live till daylight, the emperor will hear my tale and have that head of yours cut off."

Both count and lady implored the traitor Hardret, but they found no faith or loyalty in him. Seeing this, the count was deeply troubled. Charles' daughter appealed to him: "My lord," she said, "have no fear. If he tries to accuse you of anything, give him battle. You will surely win, for he is vile and treacherous."

## 42

Nothing further happened that night. In the morning, when it was light, Hardret rose and dressed. He came into the palace, sat down beside the king and made his accusation.

## 43

Hardret said: "Sire, true Emperor, I have dreadful news for you. Count Amile has dishonored your daughter: I caught her with him in the same bed. Have her burned at the stake, lord, and let her ashes be thrown to the wind. For this, by God, she must be put to death."

## 44

The emperor heard that faithless foe. "Hardret," he said, "you are very wrong to say that. Not for all the gold in Christendom would Amile be disloyal to me." The traitor said: "Send for them, then. If I cannot show the truth by defeating him in combat, order all my limbs cut off!"

Now the king was angry and deeply disturbed. No wonder! and he was hardly to blame for it. He sent for them at once, and they dared not delay.

When the king saw them, he bowed his head and showed no readiness to speak. Then he looked up at the count and said: "By God, you have made bold progress! My daughter is a rich reward for you to carry off from court. But you were caught in the act! By the apostle in Nero's Gardens, if you cannot disprove this accusation, I'll have that head of yours struck off!"

The count said: "Sire, this is a grave charge. And the man who accuses me—may a hundred curses be heaped upon his head if he fails to prove its truth!"

Hardret heard this and flew into a rage. "By God, Amile, you're a clever one! You will certainly never be caught in the act of telling the truth! Just Emperor, accept my pledge: if I cannot prove him wrong in combat, I will be hanged and dangle in the wind. And anyone be damned who tries to spare me that!"


## 45

Treacherous Hardret presented his glove; he put the gage into the hands of the emperor, and the king said: "Where now are the hostages?" At that word, sixty or more rushed forward—cousins and brothers, all kinsmen, offering themselves so no shame might befall them.

Count Amile stood in the middle of the hall; he was handsomely clad in a costly silken tunic. The king said: "Amile, what will you do? Will you confess or will you fight?" The gentle count looked at the knights, at that great crowd of Burgundians. "Lords," he said, "worthy and powerful knights, be my bondsmen before the king."

Curse the man who would offer himself as hostage for Amile!

The count saw they were silent and almost burst with wrath. He appealed to Charlemagne.


## 46

"Just Emperor, please hear me. What hostages would you have me offer? Send for my eager charger and all my arms; send for my sharp spear and my shield and steel helmet. I do not want to delay the contest any longer, but gladly undertake it here and now." And the king said: "This is a most unseemly plea. If you were now armed and on your horse, which has no peer in France or elsewhere under heaven, you would easily outrun my knights; not one of them could overtake you, and my shame would go unavenged."

He called for his sword and was going to strike off the count's head, when the queen suddenly cried out: "No, my lord, what a wicked and sinful thing! I beg you, spare the worthy count; I'll pledge my very self as hostage, and so will Belissant, on whose account the combat will take place, and so, too, my son Beuvon, whose valor is well known."

The king said: "Now I hear a proper plea. By the apostle we call pope in Rome, if he is harmed or hurt, I will have every limb of yours cut off." The count heard that and was very glad. "Ah, God," he said, "thank you, God. Now I have worthy hostages."

### 47

Count Amile was quick-witted and bold. He turned toward the king and appealed to him: "My lord," he said, "hear me: let the combat be seven months delayed." And the king said: "Willingly and gladly."

The gentle knight would surely not forget the date!

Turning toward the queen, he appealed to her: "My lady, hear me: there is one thing I must tell you. So help me God, I will not hide it: I am going to find my friend and companion, count Ami of the city of Blaye, so that he may be at the contest on the appointed day."

The queen heard this and flew into a rage: "So help me

God, I knew it!" Then she said to the count: "You are a proven coward! By the apostle in Nero's Gardens, you will not move from this good city till the battle is over which you will fight with Hardret." At this, Belissant began to weep. "Mother," she said, "let's let him go, but have him swear on holy relics that he will come free us from our bond on the day which he has set." "Daughter," she answered, "just as you wish."

The gentle count was led right off to the church. On his knees before the main altar, he was making ready for the oath, when the queen hurried in to withdraw the requirement; she ran up and raised him by the right arm. "I trust you, worthy knight." "Madam," he said, "my thanks and gratitude five hundred times over."

He went into town to his lodgings, put on his hauberk and helmet, girded his sword on his left side; he leapt into the saddle of a fresh charger, grasped a sturdy squared pike and fastened a shield around his neck. Out through the gate of the city he rode. Young Beuvon escorted him a good long way before the turning back. Off went Amile the noble and brave, off to find his friend.

## 48

Hear me, lords, and God prosper you. Here we'll take leave of Amile the brave and tell of his friend Ami, who was in Blaye in his big house.

He was sleeping in his bed, which stood on gilded legs. In the morning, at the first light of day, he was suddenly frightened and jumped up for his sword. His lady saw this and asked: "What has happened to you, gentle son of a baron?" "Lady," he said, "I'll tell you: I am afraid for my dear companion. I left him in the castle in Paris, and I am very uneasy."

## 49

"Madam," he said, "listen to this. Last night I had an awful dream that I was in Paris with Charles; Amile was struggling bravely with a lion and was up to his spurs in blood. The evil lion turned into a man, it seemed to me, and he was called Hardret. I was coming up the street; the sword was drawn which I had brought from Clermont, and with it I hacked off his head just under the chin. But by the apostle we call pope in Rome, not all the gold in this world could stop me from going off to my friend as soon as the day is bright, and with me I'll take a thousand brave knights who have pledged me their loyalty."

## 50

The noble lady appealed to the count: "My lord," she said, "I know what you're thinking. You would like to be now in the great city of Paris with count Amile, that faithless scoundrel, kissing and fondling the daughter of Charles, while I am cast aside with contempt. Oh, I wish I might hear bad news of her! I wish she would rot in foul whoredom!"

The count said: "Lady, you are very wrong to say that. By the apostle in Nero's Gardens, even to save my limbs from the axe, nothing could stop me from going off to my friend as soon as day dawns, and with me a thousand well-armed knights who won't fail me."

## 51

Count Ami was no coward, far from it, and he did not give up just because of what Lubias had said. In the morning, he rose and put on his best clothes; he had his knights handsomely equipped and swiftly set out on his way.

He is heading now toward the one man whose friend he will always be. And in a very short while, my lords, in a beautiful turn of events, he is going to find him.

## 52

Hear me, lords, and God be your friend, Christ crucified in glory! Count Amile had his hostages named; then he set right out on the road to Blaye.

He made no stop till he came to a flowered field. He sighed and exclaimed: "Blessed be the meadow which I see here, the whole field and the beautiful flowers! Here we swore and pledged our friendship, Ami and I. He has honored his oath like a valorous knight, while I have behaved like a traitor and enemy of God. But, for the beauty and flowers of this field and for the love of my steadfast friend, I will lie down and sleep here a little while. God give me back my companion Ami! I wish I had news of him, to know if he is living or dead."

He dismounted from his fine steed; he hitched the horse to a little branch and drove his sturdy gleaming spear into the ground, but he did not remove his hauberk or helmet and he kept his good shield by his head: he was in fear of his enemy Hardret and the thousand men of his clan who wanted to kill him.

## 53

Now Amile was lying in the middle of the field. Beside him stood his good swift charger, better than any in the kingdom of France; his good sharp spear stood fixed in the ground, and his strong shield lay by his head; he had not taken off his hauberk or helmet, for fear of perfidious Hardret. To one side stood an abandoned church; its walls were all ruined and broken, the towers shattered and the marble smashed. No one ever went there, for the place was too old, but the shade of the pines and the laurel was lovely. Running up to the other side was a wide road.

Count Ami, who was seeking his friend, recognized him in the field where he lay. He said to his men: "Dismount here and let your horses feed awhile. I see a peasant lying in that field. I'll go see what he is doing there and what he's about: he may be a messenger from Paris with some welcome news of my worthy companion. And yet I do want to turn back to my worthy wife, whom I left so sick the other day: there is no other such lady between here and Montpellier."

His men said: "As you wish. Go ahead, but don't delay. We must make the most of our time, for we still have a very long way to go."

## 54

Count Amile lay in the middle of the field. Before him stood his long-maned stallion; his trusted arms were there, his heavy shield and steel sword, new and sharp.

His good friend came by and recognized him as soon as he saw him. He moved aside the resting weapons lest Amile, suddenly roused, strike him by mistake. He put his right hand on the other's chest and shook him, then said: "Vassal, wake up! It's almost evening."

## 55

Count Amile straightened up. How well he knew his companion Ami! He threw his arms around him and kissed his chin a hundred times. And then they took delight in hearing each other's news.

## 56

"Dear friend," said gracious Ami, "have you seen the king this week?" "Yes, good friend, I saw him the other evening in Paris, where he was holding court. There were many Germans there and Dutchmen and men from Lorraine and Brittany and England.

"And there was Belissant, who brought her beautiful body all naked into my bed. And so it happened—I couldn't help it! But that accursed Hardret spied on me. Early the next morning, he denounced me before the king, and now I am bound to do battle with the faithless traitor. I could find no hostage, when suddenly the queen pledged me her very self, then her son Beuvon, who is valiant and brave, and Belissant, who is so lovely. I shall never see them again. A guilty man should not fight. By my sin I have killed them."

## 57

"My dear friend," said good Ami, "I told you last time at our parting and begged you in the name of holy love not to be a companion to Hardret or befriend him in any other way. He would soon bewitch and betray you, and bring you to such shame and grief as would not be easily set right."

The count answered: "In God's name, what could I do? By my faith in almighty God, Belissant, with her pure and lovely body, came to lie by my side; but that treacherous Hardret was spying on me. Early the next day, he ran to accuse me, and now I am bound to do battle with that foul traitor. But no hostage could I find, when suddenly the queen volunteered herself, then her son Beuvon, who is gracious and wise, and Belissant, with her pure and lovely body. They will never see me again. A guilty man cannot do combat. I wish I were dead!"

## 58

"Good friend," said Ami to Amile, "this battle cannot remain unfought. It shall take place, by God! And I, I tell you, by the holy Son, will fight it!"

Amile said: "Such words are senseless; the emperor has pledged his faith and sworn by the Son of holy Mary that he would accept no other man in my stead, so heartsick is he about his daughter."

## 59

Count Ami was a faultless knight, brave and wise; there has never been a better one. As soon as he heard Amile, he declared: "Dear friend, don't be distraught. Take off your clothes and put on mine; I will take that long-maned charger, all those arms and that heavy shield, and be right off to Paris as fast as I can. If that villain Hardret recognizes me during the fight, I will cut off his head, and the truth will not be known."

## 60

"Dear friend," said brave Ami, "so help me God, you're speaking madly. You and I were conceived at the same moment and born in the same night and baptized and saved at the same font. And our godfather Ysoret, so worthy of our praise, gave us gold and silver in abundance and for each of us had a goblet made. We are alike in every way; we have the same eyes, the same nose and mouth; we walk alike and ride alike, bear our arms alike. There is no man alive who, if one of has passed through a place and then the other comes, could tell the difference. Take off your clothes and wear mine, and I'll go right off to Paris. You go down there in the meadow; you will find my good knights. If they ask you why you have been so long, tell them—make no secret of it—that you were speaking to a messenger from France, who brought you news of your companion.

"Say to them, 'Now I would like to be back in Blaye.' Dear friend, when you come to Blaye and find Lubias waiting under the pine tree, she will offer you her womanhood; by the loyalty you owe me, noble baron, refuse it. If she says anything arrogant or false, raise your hand and strike her in the face. Go up into the palace then, good friend, and order that a meal be prepared of game, fowl and boar. In the evening when you go to supper, you will sit at my great table and have the steward bring in the meats; Lubias will be on your right side, count Gautier on your left. When the barons are all assembled, say to my men, those hardy knights: 'Sit, lords, as you are wont to do, for you will have food aplenty; that is my wish, by the faith I owe God.'

"When the knights have eaten, they will go to their quarters; there will be no one left in the palace. Dear friend, go to my room and Lubias will do the same. She will offer you her womanhood, and you will refuse it, my dear friend. Good companion, remain faithful to me and remember the great loyalty that each of us has sworn to the other."

So absorbed were they in their conversation that evening came and the sun was about to set. They rushed to kiss and embrace each other, and parted weeping.

## 61

Count Ami set out on his way. Count Amile went straight toward the men waiting in the grove; they ran up to him as soon as they saw him: "You have been gone long, good lord, and we have been worried." The count said: "That blessed time was all spent with the messenger; he brought me true news of my companion, that he is serving Charles and doing credit to himself. He maintains and manages the king's whole domain. Mount your horses, lords, and let's be on our way. If I were in Blaye now, I would rest, for my head is aching."

## 62

When the noble knights heard that they were on their way to
Blaye, such was their joy that I've never seen greater. Their
hearts were full of cheer. They jumped into the saddles of their
Arabian steeds and never stopped for hill or height; they did
not rest till they came to Blaye.

Lubias came forward from her tower; she recognized the
valorous knights and all the men of her father's house. In her
heart she was full of cheer. She came to meet them in the shade
of a pine tree and asked to receive her lord's sword. But noble
Amile saw her and turned away. At that, the lady thought she
would lose her senses. "Lord," she said, "you are treating me
with contempt. You are just back from court in Paris, from kissing and enjoying the daughter of Charles, and now you cast me
aside with disdain. I pray to God, our ever-truthful Father, that
I soon hear bad news of her, that she be caught up in whoredom."

The count heard her and almost burst with rage. He raised
his hand and struck her on the nose, just as his companion had
told him to do. He moved closer and tried to seize her by the
hands, as if to fling her down, but his men pulled her away.

## 63

Count Amile was noble and brave. He went up the marble steps
into the hall and ordered a meal be richly prepared of game, pork
and boar. That evening at nightfall, when they were ready for
supper, the count took his place at the great table and had the
food carried in. He asked, too, for his gold cups. Lubias sat on
his right side, count Gautier on his left. When the barons were
all assembled, the gracious count stood up and, facing the barons,
addressed them: "Sit, lords, as you are wont to do, for we shall
have food aplenty." When the night's supper was finished, the

barons went off to their quarters, as was their custom.

## 64

When they had all eaten and drunk, I repeat, they left the palace and no one remained. Count Amile went to his room and lay down all naked in his friend's bed; with him he had his keen steel sword. Lubias took off her clothes, too, and lay down naked next to the naked count, for she expected to make love to her husband. She felt the keen steel blade and jumped back in fear. God, how frightened she was!

## 65

When Lubias felt the naked sword, she was seized with fright and dread. "Lord," she said, "what have I done wrong? You have brought your sword to kill me! But by the soul of my mother, if I but live till daybreak, I will tell my cousins and brothers, and they will take me at once before the bishop. He will separate me from you and your presence!"

## 66

"God," said Amile, "by your holy name, you placed Saint Peter

at the head of Nero's Gardens and converted Saint Paul and
Saint Simon; you saved Jonah from the belly of the great fish
and Daniel from the lions' den; you protected Saint Susanna
from false witness and granted true pardon to Mary Magdalene,
just as is truly written and we believe. Now protect my dear
companion, who is in Paris in Charles' France,when he goes into
combat against that treacherous Hardret; let me see him again in
his own house." So Amile prayed in silence.

Then he turned to the lady and spoke: "Lady," he said,
"as God is our creator, I cannot love you tonight. Only the other
day, when I was with Charles as he was holding his court at Laon,
a doctor from Besançon gave me herbs and potions for a great
fever in my body and told me for thirty whole days I should not
lie with a woman or take a man's pleasure; if I do, I remain un-
healed... But by your faith in almighty God, why do you hate
my worthy friend Amile?"

"My lord," she said, "I'll tell you, and not one word will be
a lie. The other day, during Rogation Days, when the house was
full, count Amile, God curse him, right in my room tried to se-
duce me. He lifted my ermine-lined robe and was going to shame
me, but I slapped his face so hard that he fell to the floor on his
knees. That, in good faith, is the respect that he showed me, my
noble lord, and that's why I hate him."

67

"God," said Amile, "who sit on high and see all, holy Lord and
King, a man must be mad to believe a woman or to tell her any
secret he has. Now I am sure that Solomon was right: in seven
thousand, there are not four or even three perfect women to
trust."

Then he said: "Madam, you have told me the truth. Amile,
that faithless traitor, is going to die. With this sword that lies

beside me, I will hack off his head if I see him. He deserves to die."

## 68

Hear me, lords, and your lives be long! Let's take leave of count Amile and return to count Ami on his way back to Paris in the kingdom of France, there to do battle with the traitor Hardret.

Our emperor rose early in the morning and ordered a ditch be dug, broad and ample and bordered with trees. There he would dismember his wife, Beuvon his son and fair Belissant. Our emperor soon had them summoned and those who brought them forth had not dared to refuse. The emperor saw them and bowed his head; he gave them no encouraging look.

"Lady," he said, "go make yourself ready, as one does, for death. By the apostle in Nero's Gardens, your guarantor may not return in time. Unless he arrives before noon, I shall have your limbs struck off, burn you at the stake and scatter the ashes in the wind. All the gold in the world could not guard you from my fierce justice."

The lady heard and began to weep. "Lord," she said, "dear God on high, who suffered torment on the cross, save me from death and destruction, together with Beuvon my son and fair Belissant. Let that scoundrel not forever shame us."

69

The king was now distressed and grieved while Hardret was
lighthearted and pleased. He sent word to the churches to prepare for high mass. He knew full well that after midday his tri-
umph was certain. But things won't go at all as he plans!

He turned to the king and said boldly: "Just Emperor, I
will have my battle! Amile has clearly fled and will never again
return to this land. Send beautiful Belissant to the stake, and
Beuvon your son and your wife, too. Now we shall see great
justice done!... But one thing makes me wonder: that the queen
should insult me so. But what does it matter? I trust in
God, the glorious and mighty. Well before evening and the
setting sun, I'll see her burn in a blazing fire."

The lady heard and wept softly. "Ah, God," she said,
"who created mankind, you commanded father Abraham to
sacrifice his son. He was about to strike, so great was his faith
in You, when from heaven an angel flew down and seized both
the blade and the child and carried him right up to heaven to
be with the Holy Innocents in paradise. And You were born of
a Virgin in Bethlehem; there the three kings came seeking You
and brought You rich offerings: myrrh and incense and much
gold. For three years You preached to Your friends; with Your
apostles You gladly supped and then fasted long in the wilder-
ness; on Holy Thursday You gladly washed the feet of each
disciple; foul Judas, the ruthless traitor, sold You to the unbe-
lievers for a mere thirty pieces of silver; at night, by candlelight,
they captured You; there, to name You, Judas gave You his
perfidious kiss; then You were harshly nailed to the cross and
crowned by the wicked with reeds and prickly thorns; to make
You suffer greater pain, they pierced Your body with a sharp
lance, and blood gushed forth from Your side; Longinus, blind
all his life, wiped his eyes and suddenly saw; Nicodemus laid
You down gently in a large tomb; You were truly resurrected
on the third day; You harrowed hell, as is well known, and de-
livered Your faithful; You rose up to heaven to Your holy dwelling, where the traitor will never find shelter, the wicked will
never find refuge and false judges no home. As this is all true,
dear Father, glorious King—and I believe it, wretched as I am,
without any doubt—save me from death and damnation, to-

gether with Beuvon my son and my daughter Belissant. Let that scoundrel not forever shame us."

## 70

The king was now distressed and full of wrath. Hardret, that traitor—God send him down to eternal damnation!—was delighted and pleased. He turned to the king and began to speak: "Just Emperor, Amile has fled and will never be back in this land. Send to the stake my lady the queen, Beuvon your son and your daughter Belissant. Now we shall see the fruit of your justice." And the king said: "They will not escape me!"

The lady heard and sighed deeply. "Alas," she said, "God, Son of the Virgin, You ate barley bread at the last supper and gave Your disciples new strength. As this is all true, holy Mary— and I believe it, wretched as I am, without hesitation—keep me, Lady, from death and despair, together with Beuvon my son and my daughter Belissant."

Just as she finished her prayer, at the very moment of prime, she looked up and saw Ami riding up the road. She saw him and was overjoyed. She turned to Hardret with these words: "Lord Hardret, I must tell you: now you will have to bow that brazen head of yours. That head will roll today, and your belly will be pierced and run through." The great bells of Saint Victor's rang loud through the town, and all the other churches joined in to mark the hour.

## 71

When the lady had finished her prayer, she saw Ami come riding
up, ready with shield and coat of mail. She saw him and rejoiced at the sight. The lady turned to Hardret with these words:
"Now you will bow that brazen head of yours!" The good lady
berated him: "Hardret, you traitor, may God curse your soul,
that heart of yours is so full of evil! I trust in God, the Son of
Mary, that your head will roll today and your belly be pierced
and run through. You will not escape!"

## 72

Count Ami was valiant and bold, and arrived as a man neither
alarmed nor afraid. As for Hardret, he was distressed and dis-
heartened. The guards and squires ran up, and Ami, that fine
knight, dismounted under an olive tree. Our emperor saw him
and felt a leap of joy; he went up to him eagerly, as did the
beautiful queen.

They greeted Ami with great friendship, and the count
said: "I thank you, just Emperor! In the name of Jesus Christ,
our Father in heaven, let me have my battle! Let me today
champion my lady, if it please the glorious Son of God, against
Hardret, that faithless villain. With my sword of polished steel, I
am sure I can bring him down and cut off his limbs and his head,
if God comes to my aid."

## 73

Our emperor dismounted under a pine tree; a camp-chair of pure gold was brought to him, and the emperor of France seated himself. He sent right away for the relics and had them set out on a table: those of Saint Denis, almost ten of the Holy Innocents and precious relics of Saint Martin. Any man who swears falsely by them is ill-fated and can only in shame leave the field.

Noble Charles, son of Pepin, was the first to speak: "Worthy knights," he said, "I will not set aside this contest; it shall take place, by God! I would not give it up for a thousand pounds of pure gold, and there will be no further question."

Then Hardret said: "Good Lord, I agree and in front of these knights I state: whoever is defeated, let him be hanged in the morning; let there be no ransom either of silver or of pure gold, and let no family or friends intervene." The king answered: "Hardret, you have spoken well. So help me God and the saints whose relics are here, so shall it be."

But when Hardret heard the King make this solemn pledge, all his blood drained away. Now he was troubled that he had spoken too soon, for if he were defeated and brought down, he might yet have been ransomed. He seized Ami by the right hand and shouted out in a ringing voice: "Hear me, Charles, son of Pepin, and everyone else both young and old! So help me God and the saints whose relics are here and all the rest of the martyrs and confessors of the faith, this vassal, whose hand I hold here, I found in bed with Belissant, both of them naked and going madly at it like husband and wife. All worthy men must condemn him for that. So help me God, that's the way it was."

"Scoundrel," said the count, "you're lying! So help me God and all the saints whose relics are here, I have never lain or slept with Belissant, nor has her naked flesh ever touched mine. God grant me, then, to leave this field of battle alive and return home safe and sound."

Belissant was in the marble palace and through the window heard the oath. The gentle girl whispered to herself, so that no one could hear: "Ah, worthy, valorous knight, as God is my

witness, it happened just as Hardret has insisted and sworn; he
has not spoken a single lie. Dear lord Amile, may ever-constant
God protect you in his mercy and let that scoundrel not put you
to shame."

### 74

Now the two counts had taken their oaths and were running off
for their armor and weapons. Hardy knights helped Ami to prepare; he buckled his sword on his left side, hung from his neck a
strong striped shield and grasped a sturdy squared pike. He
crossed the Seine below Paris and rode into the meadow. The
king went, too, with all his fine barons, and so did the queen,
riding along on a fresh mule to watch the combat.

Powerful lords of his clan helped Hardret to prepare; he put
on his hauberk and fastened his helmet, girded his sword on his
left side and climbed into the saddle of a fresh charger; from his
neck hung his strong striped shield and in his hand he held a
sturdy squared pike. He went to cross the Seine below Paris
and ride into the meadow, but the good horse lost his footing
and stumbled, and the scoundrel was thrown.

Belissant was in the turreted castle and leaned far out
the window; in a loud voice, she cried out: "By God, traitor, the
altar is still ahead of you; you'll have to carry your offering a bit
farther!"

Hardret heard her and was stung to the quick. He got back
onto his vigorous charger and rode off to the field below Paris
where the great battle would take place.

## 75

Now the two counts were in the green meadow. On each side, they were given a wide berth for fighting. Our emperor gave his command: that neither noble nor commoner, on pain of bodily harm, utter a word till one of the fighters should declare himself vanquished.

Then they struck the steeds with their sharp spurs. Rough blows fell on the shields, the lances shattered, the saddle-bows broke—and the two counts forced each other down onto the field. Now they were both on the ground.

## 76

The counts had now both fallen over backwards; Ami stumbled first, and then that vicious Hardret. Hardret got up and Ami jumped to his feet. Hardret drew his well-honed sword; he rushed at Ami like a leaping stag and slashed at him fiercely from side to side. He tore through sixty links of his coat of mail and said: "Amile, you vile madman, I've hit you hard, haven't I? Too bad for you, all those games with Belissant under the covers!"

## 77

Anger flashed across Ami's rugged face at the villain's mean blow. He drew his gold-hilted sword and struck Hardret on the gilt band of his helmet. He sliced the right ear off his head and onto the ground, and taunted him: "By God, Hardret, you should have watched out for your ear; it won't grow back for

some time! You'll curse the day you ever saw Charles' daughter.'' He went on: "I deny with the blade of my sword that she
ever lay a single night with me and that there is any cause to
insult the good daughter of Charles."

### 78

When Hardret realized he had lost his ear, his whole body broke
into an angry sweat. He drew his bare sword from its sheath and
rushed up to Ami; with the sharp-tipped blade, he gave him—
mean greeting!—a blow aimed straight at his eye. But the count,
helped by God, moved aside in time, and the sword passed just
over the ear between helmet and head, and the point emerged
in back. Hardret struggled to pull the sword free, but it would
not come out; he gave up and paused over it no more.

All those who were watching were greatly afraid, since they
truly believed the sword had entered the head. Belissant felt
her blood run cold. "My God," she said, "what a curse that I
was ever born, since I am the cause of this battle! Better, by
God, if I had been destroyed, burnt in a blaze or stabbed dead
with knives. Ah, count Amile, God protect you today! What
has become of your valor? It used to be so feared and dreaded!
If you win now, I will be yours forever. Hardret was not wrong
to suspect my desire."

With these words, she fell down in a faint, and the faint was
so deep that people thought she was dead. Everyone, the young
and the old, wept aloud for the daughter of Charles.

## 79

Count Ami heard the news of Belissant and all the crying and wailing. His heart was moved to pity; he took hold of his polished-steel sword and with the pummel dealt Hardret such a rude blow next to the ear that his whole hand shook and the sword fell from his grasp. Hardret snatched it up from the ground and with it in hand cried out: "By God, Amile, you won't leave here alive! You'll curse the day you ever met your sweet Belissant; I'll make you pay dearly for her love!" With the sword he had snatched up from the ground, he dealt the count such an unsparing rough blow on his Pavian helmet that the sword that was embedded there fell unstuck.

Before it could reach the ground, the count seized it with a powerful grip. He could not have been more overjoyed, had he been given Pavia and the whole of the Piedmont. He turned to Hardret and shouted out boldly: "There, traitor! As God is my guardian, your sword is now mine. You'll curse the day you brought it to this field! You won't leave here alive, I can tell you! That head of yours will roll for trying to shame the daughter of Charles."

## 80

Count Ami clutched the keen sword and struck Hardret on his gleaming helmet so hard that florets and gems fell out of their settings. He cut through the hood of the Moorish hauberk, the rude blow reached the face, the right eye sprang out and hung down on the silvery front of the hauberk. The count saw it and taunted: "By God, traitor, you're not having much luck! I see you've just lost the sight of one eye. You'll curse the day you ever saw Belissant, the daughter of mighty king Charles. You are going to lose your head for this!"

## 81

Hardret was now more furious than ever as a sightless eye hung
down on his breast. With the sword that had been Ami's, he
struck the count in the chest and nearly toppled him. If not for
the hauberk which was strong and well-linked, the damnable
villain would surely have killed him. Now they were struggling
like mortal enemies as nightfall approached.

## 82

The two counts were still in the field; neither one nor the other
was winning that day. The flower of France appealed to Charles:
"Sire," said the barons, "listen to us; we wish to say a word.
Have these two lords now disarmed and let them rest until daybreak. Then you can return them with their arms to the field."
The king answered: "As you desire." And he had the com-
batants quickly parted and their weapons taken away. He did
not let them pause anywhere till they were brought within the
walls of Paris.

There their armor was fast undone and the green gem-
studded helmets were removed from their heads. Then they
went up into the princely palace. They all took their places for
the evening meal, which was plentiful and well-prepared. Count
Ami behaved like the lord that he was; after a whole day without food, he ate with hunger. But Hardret, the traitor, was
mad with fury; he could not have eaten even to save his limbs
from the axe.

The scoundrel went into a room apart and sent for one of
his godsons. He came right away, and Hardret addressed him:
"Godson," he said, "I have much loved you, yet I have neglected
one thing: I have given you no godfather's gift. Now I want to
give you a rich and noble present; it's this earnest advice: as
long as I was able to betray and denounce, Charles held me

dear and kept me privy to his secrets. Now I urge you to behave as I have done. Don't be stopped if this has been a bad day for me. My whole face is disfigured and it will not be healed for some time. But by the apostle in Rome beloved of God, Amile is dead if I can still meet him in battle tomorrow!

### 83

"I urge you, good godson Aulory, not to trouble to serve the Lord God or to tell the truth, unless you think you are lying. If you see a worthy man, be sure to insult him, and shame him with your words if you can. Burn down cities, towns and farms. Knock over and smash altars and crucifixes. Only in that way will you be honored and served."

"Have no fear, godfather," said Aulory. "It's been more than three years since I last felt any urge to do good; I am instead always ready to do evil. Don't fear, Amile is as good as dead! By God, I'm sure of that!"

### 84

Treacherous Hardret spent that night in torment until the first light of day.

Count Ami got up, put on an ermine-lined robe, went to church and made his prayer, offered that day a gold ring, and then returned to his lodgings in town. He put on his hauberk, tied on his round helmet, buckled his sword on his left side, leapt onto his Aragonese charger, and hung around his neck his lion-blazoned shield, but he took no lance, since they were all broken. He crossed the Seine by the bridge below Paris. The king went, too, and the other barons, and so did the queen on an Aragonese mule.

French knights dressed the vile traitor in his shiny hauberk and floret-studded helmet. He buckled on his gold-pummeled sword, mounted his Gascon charger, hung around his neck his lion-blazoned shield, and muttered to himself words that would doom him that day: "Yesterday I did battle in the name of the Creator. Today I will fight in the name of that lord who has never had any love for God. Ah, Devil, how triumphant you will be today!" He commended to all his body and soul. Hardret the traitor crossed the Seine.

Count Ami saw him and was seized with fear. "God," he said, "Father who created the whole world, who placed Saint Peter at the head of Nero's Gardens and converted his companion Saint Paul and saved Daniel from the lions' den—just as is truly written and we believe—grant me to slay that scoundrel, so that I may once again see my dear companion, who is in Blaye at my castle." He spoke in a whisper, so that no one could hear.

Then he drew his gold-pummeled sword, urged his horse forward with sharp spurs, and struck Hardret a great blow between hauberk and floret-studded helmet. With a single blow, he cut his head off and the faithless villain fell over onto the ground.

The king and the other barons saw it. "Vassal," said Charles, "come up to us and I shall give you my daughter."

85

Count Ami was noble and brave. He did not stop to glance at the king or pause to consider his words. He galloped down to the

Seine, crossed over and dismounted on the opposite bank. He removed his saddle and rested his horse for a while. Then he resaddled and, taking his place once more astride his mount, he leaned forward on the gilded saddle-bow and cried out in a ringing voice: "I defy you, true brave Emperor! You are offering me too poor a reward, after all the trouble caused by the lie of that traitor Hardret. If God lets me return to Blaye and find my companion, you will soon see us again right here. We will not leave you a single castle or city, not a town or village or fortress!"

Charles' knights appealed to the king: "Rightful Emperor, if you let him go and find his companion, you will soon see them right back here. They will not leave you a single tower or fortress, not a town or village or castle or city. Please make him change his mind. Give him not only your daughter Belissant but also honors and fiefs enough to win his gratitude. You were offering him too poor a reward, after all the trouble caused by the lies of that traitor Hardret, curse his soul!"

## 86

When the king had heard the words and deeds that his barons were thus urging, he made quickly for his fine steed and dashed into the river without even seeking a shallow spot. He went straight toward count Ami in a rush.

The noble count was awaiting him on the other side; the king looked at him, seized the reins of his horse and said: "Vassal, you will not move from here, except to come back with me to Paris. Brave baron, I shall be glad to have you take my daughter, and you will be my son and a brother to Beuvon."

"I will not stay," answered Ami; "this was the home of Hardret, and his many kinsmen would soon trap and kill me." The king said: "Those are wasted words. I have a thousand men for every one of them. Today, I promise you, you will see the corpse shamed and dragged through the dust."

They turned back to the castle in Paris and dismounted at the steps under the pine tree, then went up into the marble palace. Ami was quickly helped off with his armor; the green shining helmet was removed from his head, the polished steel sword unbuckled, and the tightly linked hauberk undone. He remained in his silk tunic alone.

All the fine knights rejoiced in the marble palace. God, how overjoyed they were!

87

The king summoned Ravinel de Mont Nuble, a squire of malicious nature; he was worse than others of his breed, for he had no sense at all of moderation. "Go look in every street and road, and call all your comrades together: it will be your task to destroy the body of Hardret. Let it be dragged through dust and dirt till no shred of the tunic is left. Let the head be impaled on a post and left for the crows to eat."

Then: "And you, fair Belissant, God has come to your aid. Now serve Amile as his wife and his mistress. If he betrothes you now in my presence, I shall grant him Riviers, my great city on the banks of the Dunne, where ten thousand men truly serve me whenever I need them."

## 88

The count heard this promise. "God," he prayed, "by Your holy name, You placed Saint Peter at the head of Nero's Gardens; You saved Jonah from the belly of the great fish and Daniel from the lions' den; you protected Saint Susanna from false witness, just as is truly written and we believe. Counsel me, Father of all creation! I have a wife, whom I took with the consent of my peers, and no knight in the world has one more beautiful. If I now take a second wife, God, what will become of me? Let me pledge my troth in the name of my friend; I will do penance for it to the very end, and my wife will never know."

## 89

Our emperor was noble and stern. He sent at once for the relics and had them set out on a table; there were those of Saint Denis and nearly fifteen of the Holy Innocents. He turned to the count and spoke: "Vassal, come pledge your troth to my daughter." And the count answered: "With pleasure, my good Lord, but only after I have come back from Blaye and the companion to whom I have sworn fidelity. I promise I shall return in forty days, good Sire, and then I shall do as you wish."

The King said: "That is not what I desire. You have no need to go see Ami beforehand; he is a worthy man and a noble knight, and your friendship with him will surely not suffer."

The count thought to himself: "Then I must make a false vow." And he said: "Since you wish it, I shall take my oath before your daughter. So help me God and the holy relics which are set out before me, one month from today, if God grants me to live, she will be, by His command, taken in wedlock and married."

But the king said: "That is not what I mean. *You* will take

her in wedlock, worthy and noble knight!" The count dared refuse no longer and, with a heavy heart, he pledged his troth.
Belissant heard, that gracious young lady, and whispered to herself: "God grant that you fulfill this noble promise!"

90

Do you know, my lords, what a vow is? Once a man has taken a
woman honestly to wife, he is mad if he ever breaks his sacred
word.

Once count Ami had sworn the oath, an angel came flying
down from heaven and, I'm telling you the truth, sat right down
on his shoulder. No one, neither the king nor any of his men,
could see him. He spoke into the count's ear and admonished
him harshly: "Well, Ami! how senseless you are! You have a
wife, whom you took with the consent of your kin, and no
knight or warrior has one more beautiful. Yet today you are
pledging your word to another, and God is sorely grieved. Affliction and torment of the flesh will be your lot; you will be a
loathsome leper; your eyes will dim and teeth drop out. And
from neither kith nor kin will you have any help, save from pope
Ysoret and kind Amile."

Ami answered: "There is nothing more I can do, good crea-
ture; be off now. Take my flesh whenever you will, and whatever you inflict I shall accept." Then the count turned and
said: "Fair Belissant, make your vow—I am listening." "My
lord," she said, "with no delay, just as you desire."

### 91

Charles' daughter fell to her knees. "Lords," she said, "worthy barons, recite me the oath." "With pleasure, lady," answered one of the knights. "You will swear of your own free will that you will take count Amile as your lord, with the consent of his companion Ami, and that you will never sow discord between them."

"Lord," she said, "I shall gladly so swear. So help me God and the saints whose relics are here, I shall take count Amile as my lord, with the consent of his companion Ami, and never shall I cause discord between them."

Count Ami was a worthy man and a knight; he called out to the king's men: "Lord barons, into your armor! The emperor has just granted me an escort down to Blaye!"

### 92

Our emperor was a praiseworthy man. He turned to the count and addressed him: "Vassal," he said, "such words are senseless. You will not set out from the city until tomorrow when day breaks. I will entrust to you one hundred armed knights; you can then travel safely through the countryside, without any fear of Hardret's people." The count answered: "Just as you command." Everyone then withdrew for the night.

Count Ami rose the next morning and called out to his staunch knights: "Lords," he said, "into your armor!" And they answered: "Just as you command." They saddled their well-rested horses, and Beuvon escorted them a good league's distance before turning back. Off went Ami, the noble and brave, and with him the fair Belissant.

### 93

"In God's name, sir," said Garnier, the trusted guide, "when we come to the city of Blaye, you will have a splendid and lordly wedding feast and then, when it's done, you will follow the shore straight up to Riviers and there take possession of the fiefs and domains which have been granted you."

### 94

Count Ami started out on the road that runs from Paris to Blaye. He rode through Touraine and the town of Poitiers and came one night to Saint-Jean-d'Angély. The noble knights stayed there till daybreak.

Their journey lasted so long that I cannot count the days, but one Tuesday they reached the high walls of Blaye. They saw the ships on their way from Bordeaux, with sails hoisted high on the masts. "Ever-constant God," exclaimed the count, "what a thriving city this is! May king Charles prosper, who granted me beautiful Lubias!" He dismounted from his fine steed and called out to his men.

### 95

"Lord barons," said brave Ami, "we will not enter the city today, but wait for tomorrow when the day is bright; then we

can enter in a joyous procession." They all dismounted from
their handsome horses and set up pavilions and tents. There
they would stay through the night until daybreak.

But now let's take leave of Ami and his company, and return to count Amile. At that very moment, he was thinking of
his companion and he sighed: "Dear friend, where have you
gone? Yesterday was the promised day of your return. It must
be that you're dead, slain by that traitor Hardret." Then he
looked out and in the fields below the castle saw the pitched
tents and pavilions. "My God," he said, "I have lived too long!
That must be the king come to destroy me, since Hardret was a
kinsman of Lubias. This beautiful town is so strong, though,
and guarded so well by quick young men, that I am sure the at-
tackers won't enter. But no! So help me God, that was a nasty
thought. Even at the cost of my limbs, I'll go down to speak
with them and find out who they are and from where. I would
rather die than not go, since my companion has met his death
for me. Wretch that I am, I will never see him again."

## 96

Count Amile was noble and bold. He put on his hauberk and
helmet, buckled on his sword and straddled his mount; from his
neck hung a quartered shield and he was holding a sturdy sharp
spear. He told no one where he was going, no guard or squire
or even Lubias. He hurried out through the gate.

Count Ami was sitting in his camp; Charles' daughter held
him in her arms, but he had no desire to kiss her or embrace
her. When the companion whom he held so dear rode up on his
swift charger, Ami recognized him at once. "Vassal," he said,
"you are very bold indeed! Are you challenging us for your
city?"

Amile heard this and at once knew his friend. He galloped

up to him, jumped down from his quick horse, tore off the straps of his striped helmet and let his silvery hauberk drop to his feet. The two men rushed forward to kiss and embrace and take delight in hearing each other's news.

97

The two counts were sitting in the field. No man in God's creation would not have been moved to see how they embraced and rejoiced in each other. "In the name of God, sir," said count Ami, "Hardret is dead; I have killed him for you. And now I have brought you beautiful Belissant. You will marry her, for so said the king." Amile heard and was happy. The two men fell again into each other's arms.

"In God's name, sir," said count Amile, "my own news is brief: I have lain down to sleep beside your wife; her beauty has no peer in sixty countries. I wonder how you could stay away so long!" At this, Ami gave him a smile, and the two friends once more kissed and embraced.

The daughter of Charles sighed deeply and said: "Lords, by all the holy saints, you are so much alike in every way—with the same gait, with the same mouth and eyes and face—that I can't tell which of you is my husband." At that, Ami gave her a smile and whispered in her ear: "As God is my witness, madam, my companion here is your husband. If I have misled you, it was not as a foe." "In the name of God, sir, no—as a very brother! I am honored by you."

## 98

They parted that night until daybreak, when Belissant was led
to the church and count Amile wed her. With no delay everyone
then went up to the castle, and all those worthy mothers' sons
made a great feast for the count and his bride.

## 99

They parted that night until dawn, when the tents and pavilions
were taken down and the mules and pack-horses were loaded
again with gold and silver and costly robes. Then they passed
through the gate into the city, and Lubias came out to meet
them. She saw Ami and questioned him: "Who are these people
coming along the streets?" The count said: "Lady, do not be
troubled. These are the men of white-bearded Charles, whom
you will welcome in friendship if you care at all for me."

"With pleasure, my lord, on condition you let me lie in bed
with you tonight without your naked sword between us." The
count answered: "Yes, lady, now it is perfectly fitting. The pains
and fever I had were great and affected my whole body, but now,
thanks to God, they have left me and fled."

Meanwhile, Belissant was stepping down from her mule,
and Lubias went forward to meet her. They greeted each other
courteously—but their friendship, I can tell you, would be
broken before evening and the end of the day. Then they all
went straight up to the feast in the palace. There were peacocks
and cranes aplenty, and jongleurs playing their vielles and tam-
bourines. Never had such joy been seen as the joy of Belissant's
wedding.

## 100

Count Ami went to his bed; beside him lay his wife Lubias. Once they had enjoyed and delighted each other and done all that man and wife may do, the wicked woman began to speak: "My lord," she said, "I am very surprised at your dear companion Amile, who fought with Hardret a short while ago. One of his servants has admitted to me that he had a crossbow in the battle and sinfully shot Hardret with an arrow in the head; he toppled him dead from his quick charger. Count Amile came galloping up and, drawing his sword, hacked off his head and left it on the ground. But by the apostle we call pope in Rome, if I live until daybreak, he won't leave here with his mules and horses, for I'll have him thrown into a dungeon. I am mistress of this city!"

## 101

Count Ami was upright and loyal; he could not bear to hear such insults hurled at his companion. In the morning, as soon as it was light, he went to the inn of Gautier and roused his friend. "Lord," he said, "wake up at once! Have your men make ready to leave. Set out right away for Riviers, I implore you. Go take possession of your castles." And the other answered: "Just as you say."

He hurried to rise and dress, and had his men make ready to leave, then took the main gate out of the city. Off went Amile, upright and loyal. His dear companion escorted him two good long leagues and then turned back, but not before they had clasped each other in a close embrace. They parted in tears.

## 102

Off went Amile, heroic and bold, and with him the daughter of
Charlemagne. They traveled through strange lands and towns,
and came at last to the rapid waters of the Dunne. They board-
ed great dromonds and barges. The knights all sailed and rowed
together, and they soon reached the gates of Riviers. Those in-
side were overjoyed to see the new lord of their city.

## 103

Now Amile was in Riviers. The people pledged him their loyalty,
for they recognized fair Belissant and the king's barons.

But let's take leave of Amile and return to count Ami, the
valiant lord of Blaye. The words of the angel had come true.
His nose had become sunken and sore, and his tongue had grown
thick, but it was some time before the count's disease was sus-
pected. Then Lubias, that wicked, damnable woman, conceived
such hatred for him that she refused any longer to look at him
or touch him or offer him her body; she was heedless of God.

## 104

One Sunday, when night had fallen, count Ami went to bed and
called to his wife Lubias: "Come lie and sleep with me, madam."
"My lord," she said, "I'll come to you gladly."

Fully clothed, she sat down by the count and spoke her wily words: "My lord," she said, "I wonder at what has happened. You married me seven years ago, when you were healthy and well; now I see you are so utterly weak that you can no longer walk or ride. I am asking, then, that we be parted with the bishop's consent; you would be kind to agree."

The count could not believe his ears. "Madam," he said, "you have lain in wait for me and overwhelmed me and struck me down. You bring to mind the fool and the bird on the branch: the fool sits under the tree, waiting to catch the bird whole, alive and intact. He would do better to stone it down, pluck its feathers and have it readied to eat. That's how you are, by my head! I thought I could serve and honor the lady I had taken as wife. Now I see you are so utterly brutal and cruel that I must appeal to glorious God in heaven to save and avenge me."

## 105

Now Lubias answered Ami: "My lord," she said, "your response is too harsh. Do you think you can lie here in anger and rant and rave to God? Only as long as He wants is a man healthy, and death, too, comes when He wants. Even before the end of March or April, everyone who sees you, young and old, will say that your body is rotting and sick. They'll see the leper you are, I tell you. Neither kinsmen nor friends will offer you help, and you will have to run away from this land." Still fully clothed, Lubias left the bed. God, how embittered she was!

## 106

That night Lubias left him until the next day when the sun came out. She summoned two knights of her court to take the count before the bishop. There she denounced and attacked Ami and humiliated him.

Had she but served him and cherished and loved him, she would have earned saintly glory. Husband and wife are but one flesh and must never be disjoined.

## 107

Lubias said: "My lord bishop, my husband is ill and leprous. Decree a separation between us, and I will give you, holy bishop, my Arabian mule and thirty Parisian pounds."

"True God," said the bishop, "dear loving God, how astounding these words are! Even if the whole world thought him and called him a leper, you as his wife should deny it and hide it. So help me God the King of paradise, not by me will Ami be destroyed!"

## 108

Lubias, wild with fury, turned against the bishop of the city: "This city is mine, and mine is the power; this land is under my command. No bishop can deny my will; no man here has authority over me. Put down the crosier; I forbid you to bear it anymore."

"No, by my faith, lady, I will not! If you are displeased with Ami, leave his bed, but do not leave him. Keep that vow at least, for you have betrayed all the others."

## 109

Lubias was at strife with the bishop, and news of it soon reached the whole town. Nor was there anyone left who could not plainly see the state of Ami. As he went through the streets, the townspeople whispered: "Look at lord Ami, friend; how broad his nose is, how swollen his lips! How twisted his mouth is! Our lady is right: her marriage has gone amiss."

Lubias, for her part, was seeking allies through the city. To powerful men she gave money, and she dressed merchants in fur. They then went to the church and all together cried out to the bishop: "Why have you humiliated our lady and forced a leper on her?"

"By God," said the bishop, "how wrong you are about her! Someone else, not I, will have to meet your demand. Let my lady be ready tomorrow morning. Let the matter be brought before three other bishops, who will gather here at the hour of prime. Let count Ami be present at the hearing in the great hall. So help me God the glorious Father, not by me will he be destroyed!"

## 110

In the morning, when dawn appeared, there was a great throng

before the four bishops. They all went up to count Ami in the
main hall and addressed him with respect: "Gentle lord, how
ill you are! Your whole body and all your limbs are burning like
fire. It was God's will that you become a leper. When you die,
may your soul be saved!"

"God," said the count, "I accept my fate, but beseech
Lubias, so hearty and strong, that, for the love of our heavenly
Father, she build me a shelter on her land outside Blaye's walls,
near the gate, and that she grant me the crumbs from her table,
so that I not die in hunger and pain. That would be a great act
of charity."

### 111

The highest lords and the most noble princes all together that
day begged Lubias that out of charity she grant the count sustenance. She promised at once in the presence of all. May God
our glorious Father bring her to shame, for she soon broke her
word. God curse her soul!

### 112

Count Ami, with knights all around him, leaned against the high
table where the bishops were sitting. "Lords," he said, "please
hear me. I came to this good city seven long years ago; only too
soon, a sin brought me low with my affliction. The very king
who rules France gave me for wife the graceful and lovely Lubias
you see. She is young and desires enjoyment of life; but if she
goes beyond what is proper, in the name of God admonish her.

I have a son, too--agile and lively young Girard. Hold him dear; from him you will hold your domains and your fiefs. And if there is any nobleman or commoner, any deacon or provost or anyone else who has betrayed his allegiance or sinfully broken his vow of fealty, as men sometimes do to their rightful lord, in the name of Jesus I forgive him that sin; may he do likewise for me, for I can ask no more of any man here."

Lubias, faithless wife, swooned at the words of the valiant knight. When she revived, she loudly exclaimed: "My gentle lord, you are leaving us in so much grief!" At this, the barons echoed: "Ah, valiant count, how sad we are to see you leave, how sorrowful and pained and brokenhearted!" With that, a number of them felt faint for love of Ami.

Lubias took an old hut that stood just outside of Blaye and had it repaired to shelter count Ami. The churchmen all escorted him there in a great procession and then turned back to the city. God, what heartache and grief!

## 113

Now Ami was all alone in the hut, brokenhearted and suffering and sick, with no one there to care for him and keep him company. Only his son Girard gave any thought to him; he was only seven years old, very young indeed, yet he was stout-hearted enough to take bread when he could from the table and carry it out beyond the walls to his father in the hut.

His mother found out. She berated him and threatened; she threw him to the ground and slapped him and beat him till you could see welts on his body. "Leper's child, son of a cripple and beggar! I won't let a day go by without a thrashing. I won't let a month pass after Easter without getting a stepfather after you. And he'll have to be a coward not to kill you for this love of your father!"

### 114

Young Girard ran across the room and jumped onto a table:
"Listen to me, lord greybeards! My mother's treachery was
great; my father's disease would never have been known, so help
me God, if not for her tongue. Any man here who agrees she
should beat me is a bastard and a faithless traitor!" He looked
around and saw a big club; he picked it up as well as he could
and struck four men on the head.

The old men ran out, saying to one another: "He's grown
up fast! God above protect him: he's the one from whom we'll
hold our domains."

### 115

Young Girard ran down the steps and hurried into the kitchen.
He found a peacock there, roasted and well seasoned. He turned
to the cook and cried out: "Bastard, you hateful scoundrel!
You've fast forgot my father. He hasn't eaten since Monday at
noon and now it's Thursday; a long time has gone by. Go at
once and take him this peacock." The cook answered: "That
would be madness. Your mother would have me killed right
away." Girard heard this and flew into a rage; he looked around,
found a big stick, and struck the rascal across the back. Then he
dealt him a terrible blow right between forehead and nose, and
smashed his brains into the coals. He said: "So much for you,
scoundrel! That's how things are done!"

The other two cooks saw all this and were terrified. They
called out to Girard: "Strong young lord, we'll go, if you order
us to." And Girard answered: "That was well said." All three
put together and packed provisions for Ami and took them to

the count in his shelter. They gave him water to wash, and brave young Girard served him his food.

"Eat, dear father. Much time has passed since I last came to you; so help me God who suffered on the cross, I was kept away against my will." Girard, the bright young lord, told how his mother had treated him in the castle. The count, hearing this, began to weep. Girard kissed him on the mouth and nose. "Son," said the count, "stand away from me. The disease that afflicts me is so dreaded by the world that no living being or mother's son fails to turn away at my approach, for fear of my poisonous breath."

The young man said: "Such words are senseless. Your body can never disgust me; it is dear to me and good and beautiful. By the apostle in Rome whom God loves, if you decide to flee from here, I will go with you if I am not kept back; you will never find a more loyal man than me. I will beg for food and bread in the name of God; I would willingly do it."

## 116

"Son, I will go away, but I don't know when. You will remain and become a knight and keep your dignities and fiefs."

Girard left when his father had eaten. His wicked mother abused him and kicked him and hurled him to the ground. She summoned two knights, had them take and bind him by force and had him locked up in the tower.

Now the lot of count Ami grew worse, with starvation at hand, for he would have nothing to eat unless God were to take pity on him.

## 117

One Sunday, early in the morning,Lubias rose and dressed. She summoned two knights and, escorted, went outside the walls of Blaye to hear mass and matins at the church of Saint Michael. Before her walked a jongleur from Poitiers, playing his vielle and singing of love and friendship. If she had heeded his words, she would have profited by them!

The leprous count heard them passing and, as well as he could, rose and dressed. He stepped out to meet them in the middle of the road, but, too weak to stand, he sat down on the ground. · As they drew near, he pulled himself up with his stick and called out as well as he could: "Lubias, lady, hear me, please. When you cast me outside the walls of Blaye, you promised me, as God is my witness, that I would not want for food. But now this wretched beggar is dying of hunger: I am starving to death, so help me God. Let me hope, madam, for the crumbs that fall from your table tonight. Your dogs and hunting hounds feed on them now; couldn't you send them to me instead? It would not be a foolish or wrong thing to do."

Hearing this, the faithless woman answered: "My dear leper, you are tiring me. How quickly you've learned to beg! When I cast you out of Blaye, my stewards and knights assured me you wouldn't live long, but die soon; yet now I see you are healthy and well. I hope the great Judge of heaven will not grant you another month's life. How tiresome you are!"

## 118

She called upon townsmen and knights: "Lords," she said, "please advise me. This leper will kill me if he's not stopped. I

give you my word, he wants everyone to be a leper like himself."
One of the knights, God on high curse his soul, took her aside
and said: "My lady, please hear me; I shall give you good advice.
Have it proclaimed that no man, neither knight nor townsman
nor anyone else, ever have anything more to do with Ami or give
him food enough to live even one night. I give you my word,
he'll soon die." The faithless woman said: "That is very good
advice."

She summoned her herald, Bricaudel d'Orléanais: "Go and
proclaim that no man, neither knight nor townsman, ever have
anything more to do with Ami or give him food enough to live
even one night." Now he would die of hunger and thirst, our
worthy well-born count.

## 119

There's Bricaudel now, crying through the city and proclaiming
in his bold and ringing voice: "In the name of my lady, I proclaim that no one, neither squire nor servant nor knight, neither
man nor child, ever have anything more to do with Ami or give
him a single farthing."

He'll surely die now unless God takes pity on him!

## 120

Ami remained alone in his hut, and no one dared come near him,
since Lubias, God curse that evil woman, had forbidden it.
There were two serfs, though, whom the count had bought for

good money in earlier days. They went before Lubias and said: "My lady Lubias, by all the saints in heaven, it is a sin, so help me God, to let that gentle man die of hunger. Give us leave to serve him. We shall take him to foreign lands and there, we swear to God, we'll beg bread and wine and meat for him."

The wicked woman said: "You have my leave. If you do as you have said and take him out of this town and this land so that I never see him again, I will give you my Arabian mule and thirty Parisian pounds." The two men pledged their word. Lubias gave them the money as she had promised and gave them her Arabian mule as well. And they were both very happy.

### 121

Garin and Haymon were noble and good. The next day, they arose at the hour of prime and went to the count's shelter. They saw Ami and said gently: "Rise now, fair kind lord. Our lady, who used to be dear to you, has said that you may no longer stay in this city. We shall take you away to Saint Gilles and there, in the name of the Father and the Son born of Mary, we'll beg bread for you. We'll gladly do it."

### 122

Garin and Haymon were brave and true. They dressed him in haste and let the news be known through the city. There was great sorrow among townsmen and knights, and forty or more collapsed in a faint.

Noble count Ami made his way up to the castle. Steadying himself against the high table, the weak count said: "Lubias, listen to me. Show me my son Girard one last time, for I will never see him again in my life." The faithless woman answered: "That's a foolish wish, and I find it vexing to hear you. How tiresome you are!"

## 123

"Lubias, in the name of the saints in God's heaven, show me my son Girard one last time, for I will never see him again in my life." The faithless woman said: "That's a foolish thought. By the apostle in Rome whom God loves, if you don't leave my palace at once, I'll have you thrown out like a beggar." At this, the count began to weep. "O God," he said, "where can I go, if the woman who should have loved me now fails me?"

He staggered down the marble steps to a waiting mule, and the two servants helped him into the saddle. All the people of Blaye were there. They would have given him fine gifts and loaded the mule with silver and gold if it had not been forbidden by Lubias, that wicked woman, God curse her! As Ami took the main gate out of the city, his serfs turned to him and asked: "Dear kind lord, which way shall we turn?"

"Friends," he said, "take me to Rome, to my godfather, Ysoret. He will not fail me as long as I live." The servants heard this and were overjoyed. They asked the right way and traveled all day until dark, when they stopped for the night in Montramble. God lead them safely on their journey!

## 124

Count Ami set out on his way and took the straightest road to Rome. The mountains were steep and the peaks were high; the deep valleys were a terrible foe. The travelers were in great danger and thought they would die. But then, not a moment too soon, they saw Monjeu. They rested there for three days and regained their strength, and on the fourth day they set out once more on their journey. Now they came to Lombardy.

## 125

Garin and Haymon were brave and wise. They led their lord gently as he sat on the mule and, passing Monbardon, they spent countless days on the road—what they went through, I can't tell you—till they saw the high walls and towers of Rome. At Monjoie, count Ami got down from his mule and sent Haymon to speak to his godfather.

Haymon went without a moment's delay and found Ysoret standing on the high porch of the palace. He greeted him with these words: "God save you, my lord—Jesus Christ born of Mary in Bethlehem and nailed to the cross. I am sent to speak to you by a leprous count; he is called Ami and was born in Clermont. For love of God, he asks that you take him in and give him a cloak or a coat or a cape; don't let the cold winter kill him."

"God born of woman," said the pope, "dear sweet Jesus, blessed be Your name! Of all the men in Christendom, so help me God, he is one that I love most." With relics and crosses and censers, Haymon and many others returned to count Ami and in a great joyous procession led him into the city. Now Ami was in Rome.

### 126

Ami was now at the court of his godfather. There was nothing he needed that he did not have right away, save good health, which he longed for above all.

But that, I can tell you, was on its way, too.

His two men served him nobly and bravely for three whole years with no thought for themselves. But then the good and true pope reached the end of his life, and famine came to the people of Rome. They all hurried away from the city, noblemen and commoners alike. Ami was now left without sustenance.

### 127

The noble count called his two serfs: "Lords," he said, "what will become of us? The pope is dead, and we have suffered a great loss. Now take me back to Clermont in Auvergne. There in my home I have two brothers, knights in their own right, and two sisters, unwed when I left. They will not fail me, even if it costs them their lives."

At these words, the servants readied their mules and helped count Ami into his saddle. They traveled through towns and villages and fields, and made no stop until they reached Clermont. Now the count was in his own town.

### 128

Ami was now in the city of Clermont. Outside their door, he found his brothers amusing themselves at checkers and dice. He threw his arm around Hoedon, the elder: "Brother," he said, "look at me. We all three have the same father, and the same mother gave birth to us all. Build me a shelter and give me a cloak or a coat or a cape; don't let the cold winter kill me. Yours will be the reward."

### 129

Hoedon spoke up—God! how could he speak that way? "Leper," he said, "keep your distance. Confound the man who ever gives you a glance! And by God, don't think you're any longer a brother of mine."

Then lord Ami woefully turned to an old white-haired knight, who recognized him by his face and his gear. The old man stepped forward to embrace him, and so did the others standing by. They would have received him well and offered fine gifts, and he would never again have been poor, if not for his brothers.

### 130

The younger brother went up to Hoedon, knelt close and spoke his mind: "In the name of God, sir, this is Ami of Clermont, who left us this fine house when he entered the service of Charles. Send him away; let him sell his ermine-lined robes and spend all

the gold and silver he has acquired from rich king Charles.
There's no need to give him support!"

### 131

Now listen to me, young and old. The younger brother rose to
his feet. He knew very well that Ami had been recognized by all.
He turned to him and said: "Leper, you have a very fine mule.
You can sell it whenever you like; it will bring you at least sixty
sols, even more. With such a sum you can go a good long time."
He stepped up to the mule, took hold of the bit and pushed it
deep into the animal's mouth. The mule took fright, and Ami
fell down so hard that blood spurted out of his mouth and nose.

At that, the two servants ran up; each of them angrily seized
a stick and they were going to strike the two brothers, when the
count cried out: "Stand away! Leave those fools; they surely
know no better. May God forgive them."

### 132

Garin and Haymon were noble and loyal. They helped their
lord back onto the mule and turned toward the road, leaving
the marble palace on their right. "God," said the count, "where
can I turn? Glorious Father who were nailed to the cross, now I
know well that I have no friends." God, how sadly he wept!

### 133

Ami moved off, his once-rugged face now covered with tears. He turned to his servants and spoke: "Lords," he said, "by the souls of your fathers, your great faithfulness has surely won you a place in heaven. Go back now to your own country. My riding is done; the flesh has come away from the bones of my legs."

"Lord," said Haymon, "why did you keep it from us? I would have made you a litter, and we would have carried you through all those foreign lands." The servants bought a cart for three sols and lined bottom and sides with fresh grass and reeds; gently they lifted in lord Ami and then hitched up the mule. People came up from every side; they would have offered fine gifts and filled the cart with silver and gold, if not for those three faithless brothers, God curse them!

### 134

Garin and Haymon were loyal and good. They led their lord through many broad lands, taking the road that went through Bourges and from there straight into Berry. They found famine and need all along their route; they had to spend what they had, had to sell their few furs and even the Arabian mule.

One day they came upon a pilgrim, who showed them the right way.

135

Garin and Haymon called out to the palmer: "Brother, good friend, do you know of any land where we could find enough to eat?" "Yes, indeed, sir," answered the palmer, "but I must tell you that it's far from here. You have to follow the coast all around Brittany as far as Mont-Saint-Michel. There you will find such plenty that you can buy four loaves of bread for a penny."

At that, the serfs were overjoyed and took heart. They started to drive the cart forward themselves, one pulling in front and the other pushing behind, taking the road by the sea all around Brittany till they reached Mont-Saint-Michel.

There they found those treacherous sailors! Count Ami leaned against the side of the cart and called to the head boatman: "Lord," he said, "hear me, please. I am sick and need comfort and help. In the name of our glorious God, I pray you, ferry me across the water." The treacherous sailors answered: "Even if you were healthy and well, you would have to wait a good long time to get across."

"Scoundrels," said Haymon, "God confound you! My lord is a count who once had a thousand knights, and we are bound in his service." Hearing this, the vicious boatmen stepped up to the side of the cart and addressed the count: "Noble lord, sell us one of your men!"

The count heard these words and shook with anger. "Scoundrels," he said, "God confound you! These two men have carried me through the world and, if not for them, I would be helpless." "My lord," said Haymon, "do it, I beg you. To save himself a man may surely sell or pawn a thing that he owns."

Despite Ami's plea and his love, Haymon gladly traded himself to the cruel boatmen for one hundred silver marks, for bread and wine and fish, and for passage across the water. They honored their bargain right away: they put the money into the coffer, carried Ami aboard the ship and gave him food and drink. Then they let out their lines and hoisted the sails. The wind rose, making the sails billow forth, and carried the travelers along like a bird.

But the treacherous sailors fell into a quarrel. The captain said: "I'll take the gain of the bargain with that sickly vassal." And the others answered: "What you're claiming is mad! All five of us are going to share it." At this, the captain almost burst with rage. They all came to blows, striking out madly with sticks and oars. Three men drowned and two were knocked dead, so that only Ami remained on board alive, he and his two upright servants.

They did not know what to do.

### 136

"Ever-true God," said Ami, "let me not perish before I see my dear companion." "My lord," said Haymon, "don't be worried. This is not our first brush with the dangers of the sea. Garin will take the rudder and I'll man the oars."

Our ever-true God granted them to reach the other side in two weeks. The two servants carried Ami out of the boat. They could see houses to their right past a low hill, but they could not know they were seeing the princely town of Riviers, the city of the dear companion.

Count Amile was sitting down for the evening meal. He summoned his steward Remy: "Take care," he said, "that everyone is well served." "My lord," said the steward, "just as you desire."

Suddenly, there at the door, shaking his leper's rattle and seeking a gesture of kindness, stood the valiant count Ami.

Amile heard him as he sat eating and called to Remy: "I

hear a leper at the door. In the name of the Lord, go, take him
bread and wine and meat. May God see me and give me back
my companion Ami, and let me hear news of him and know if
he is living or dead."

The steward took the bread and the wine and ran down the
marble steps to count Ami.


### 137

Count Ami took the bread and the meat, while Garin and Haymon held out his goblet. The steward did not hesitate to pour in
the wine he had brought and fill it to the brim, yet he could not
help wondering. He ran up the steps of the palace and spoke to
his lord.


### 138

"You sent me down to the worthy leper. Though he is sick,
there is no one more fair under heaven. He has a goblet which
is much to be admired; if it were set alongside yours, no man in
God's creation could tell one from the other."

"Take me to him, brother," answered the count. And the
other said: "By my head, with pleasure!" Count Amile wasted
no time, eager as he was to see his companion at once. But they
failed to find him, because Ami had gone off to Saint-Michel outside the walls.

## 139

Amile and his man ran down the steps of the castle, but found no one at the gate below: Ami had gone to the town outside the walls to beg for more bread. Count Amile rushed after him, saw the cart and the servants beside it. He gripped the shaft and asked: "Lord, where do you come from?"

And Ami said: "What concern is it of yours? Can't you see that I am a leper? I am in search of Amile, whom I long for, but I cannot find him. I am deeply distressed and wish I could die."

## 140

Count Amile heard the voice of Ami, his friend and longed-for companion, and jumped into the cart to throw his arms around him and kiss him.

Then he led him back up to the castle and gave him, in the place of honor, a seat of rare green African silk. At that, beautiful Belissant questioned her lord: "Who is this man, my lord? Don't keep it from me, for I see you are happy and I would like to share in your joy." "Madam," he said, "in the name of holy charity, this is my friend, whom I love very dearly, my companion, who saved me from death and destruction."

Belissant heard and was overjoyed; she embraced him and kissed him, kissed his face and his mouth and his nose. What joy there was that evening!

## 141

The daughter of Charles knelt down beside Ami. "Ah, noble son of a venerable man," she said, "I saw how bravely you fought in the combat with that ruthless Hardret. You will never again want for a bed, for you and my lord are comrades-in-arms and you saved us from death."

## 142

Now Ami was back with his friend, in a house filled with strength and well-being and joy. And there was nothing he lacked or longed for, save good health.

One night as he lay in his flower-painted room, an angel of our Lord came in and sat down on the marble floor. He called to him with loving gentleness: "Dear sick lord, do you have any strength?" Ami heard his voice just as he saw his light and radiance and great splendor, and offered thanks to our Lord Jesus. Then he spoke tenderly to the angel: "Who are you, please, whom I hear calling? In the name of God, speak again!"

## 143

The angel said: "Have you any strength left? Have you even one limb which is whole and untouched?" Ami answered: "I won't deny I still have one arm I can use. It used to be that in the thick of battle I could really brandish a sword, but now I pray God who rules all that He let me not live much longer as I am."

## 144

The angel said: "Do not be frightened by what I am going to say. Tomorrow will be Sunday, the holy day of rest, when everyone goes to church in the morning to matins and mass. Fair Belissant will go, but you will not; you will stay here, and her lord, your loving friend, will come here to see you. Then you will tell him that God has sent word of your cure: if he were willing to behead his children, those two fine boys that he loves so much, and then bathe your body in their blood, you would be healed and made well. There is no other way, but this way will not fail."

## 145

When the good angel had given his message, he departed without a moment's pause and rose to heaven with a hymn. The rest of the night, Ami lay in fever and anguish over the news.

At the first light of day, count Amile woke brightly from his sleep, and so did lovely Belissant, the best lady in any land you might name. While she went to pray at Saint Simon's, count Amile went to his companion's room. He found him awake and greeted him: "Ami, dear brother, how are you today?" Ami answered: "I shall be well if God Almighty wills it."

## 146

"Ami, good brother," said the valiant count, "can you rise at all from your bed? I would gladly take you to church and carry you tenderly in my arms. I love you dearly, by Saint Clement! You risked your life in the contest with that evil Hardret, and it was all for my sake. The pair we are will soon be split apart, for your body is fast growing weak. By my faith in all-powerful God, if I knew of anything in this world which might bring you comfort, if I had to sell or pawn anything or anyone I have, even Belissant or my two dear sons, I swear I would do it."

Ami heard these words and was moved to the depths of his being. The tears of his heart rose to his eyes, and he cried. He praised glorious and all-powerful God, for now he knew well—he had heard and seen and understood—that he would yet recover his life.

## 147

Count Amile saw Ami weeping; it grieved him, and he offered comforting words: "Dear sweet friend, in God's name, don't despair. I will not fail you as long as I live. If I could imagine any remedy, were I even to lose all my lands in order to bring you back to health, I pledge my word I would do it at once. Only in need does a man know who is his friend and who loves him."

Gentle and noble Ami said: "If I dared utter what I know and you were willing to heed my words, then, if you wished, you could heal me and cure my body and restore me to myself. I tell you this without fear."

## 148

Count Amile heard these words, heard that he could help. He knelt down and made himself humble before God; he prayed to the Son of Mary and then said: "Friend, do not hide it from me; tell me your secret at once."

"I cannot, sir; you would not do it, but would think it madness, I'm sure, an outrage and crime. I would not tell you for all the gold in Russia; I would rather remain a leper and suffer and waste away."

"Friend," said the other, "then now you don't love me. I beg you, by God the Son of Mary, who raised Saint Lazarus from the dead in Bethany and for us all suffered great torment when His body was nailed to the cross and on the third day conquered death, I beg you, by the faith we pledged each other and by the friendship we have kept unsullied and true, tell me your secret; tell me how you can be helped and made well. Even if I have to abandon all my goods on this earth and every day of my life go begging my bread from abbey to abbey, you will be restored to health."

## 149

Ami answered: "You have begged me to tell you. Do not now think it wrong or rebuke me, good friend, if I do; and in the name of God, please do not blame me if you choose not to act. Last night, in the darkness, as I lay in this soft bed, an angel clothed in brightness came to me from our Lord Jesus. He spoke of many things; he asked, and had to know for certain, whether ever again I wanted to regain my health. And I answered: 'I prefer to die.' Then he told me not to be afraid, not to despair.

### 150

"The angel said: 'Listen to me,' and so I did, without uttering
a word. He told me—I can no longer hide it—that I should ask
if you would take your two sons, Moran and Gascelin, whom you
love so much, and behead them, then collect their blood in a
bowl and in that blood wash my body; only so would I regain
my health."

The count heard and began to weep. He did not know what
to do; he could not utter a word. He was stung, and sadness
filled his heart: how could he kill, how could he slay those two
sons that he had fathered? If it were known, who could guard
him from punishment and shame? But then he thought, too, of
Ami whom he loved so dearly: how could he let him be doomed
and deny him his help, just when his friend was so close to a
cure?

It is an awesome thing to bring a man back from death, yet
a terrible act to slay two children; no one can forgive such a sin,
save almighty God, who suffered for His Son.

"God who hold us in Your hands," said Amile, "this man
risked his life for my sake in the combat with treacherous Hardret. If I can return him to life through my very own flesh,
the true children of my holy vows, blessed be the hour of their
birth! If my companion can recover that which no man alive
may give him except with the help of almighty God who holds us
in His hands, then, even to save my limbs from the axe or to
have all the gold in the world, I must not fail to sacrifice my two
sons and come to the aid of Ami.

## 151

"Ami, my dear companion, can it be true, what you have told me? Will you be made well by my sons when you are bathed in their blood? Your wish will not be denied."

With that, Amile rushed out of the room and into the great hall. He ordered out all those who were there, guards and pages and knights, and the hall was deserted. He shut and barred the doors, and ran all around from room to room to make sure that no one was left. When he saw that he was all alone in the palace and could act without being seen, he took his sword and a golden bowl and went straight to the room where the two boys were lying side by side.

He found them asleep in each other's arms: their beauty had no match even as far as Duurstede. He gave them a long and tender glance. His distress was so great that he fell to the floor in a faint, and with him fell the sword and the golden bowl.

When he came to himself, the good knight sighed: "Wretch that I am, what can I do?"

## 152

Count Amile was distraught and bewildered. He dropped to the floor in a faint, and with him dropped the bowl and the bare steel sword.

When he recovered his senses, he said: "Amile, wretch that you are, born to behead your own children! Yet what does it matter, if my deed will rescue a man who is scorned by the world and regarded as dead? Now he will be brought back to life!"

### 153

Count Amile faltered for a moment. He stepped slowly up to the children; he found them asleep and gazed at them for some time.

He raised his sword and was about to kill them, but could not yet strike. The older boy had awakened in fright when the count had come into the room. The child turned and saw his father; his glance fell on the sword, and he was seized with fear. He called to his father and said: "Dear father, in the name of God who created the world, what are you going to do? Don't keep it from me. No father has ever done what I fear you are thinking."

"Dear son, I am going to kill you and your brother sleeping beside you, for the blood of your bodies can heal my generous companion Ami, who is an outcast in this world."

### 154

"Dear sweet father," said the boy right away, "if your companion can be healed with the blood of our bodies, do with us as you will; you gave us life, and we are your flesh. Cut off our heads quickly and let us stand before God. We will go singing up to heaven and pray to all-loving Jesus that He protect you from sin, you and your noble companion Ami. Remember us, in the name of almighty God, to our mother, fair Belissant."

At this, the count was moved to the depths of his being and again fell to the floor in a faint. When he came to himself, his courage returned.

Now, good listeners, you're going to hear such a marvel that you could never have imagined its like in your life. Count Amile stepped up to the bed and, as he raised the sword, his son stretched forth his neck. It's a wonder his heart didn't fail him—but the father brought the blade down on his child and collected the blood in the shining silver bowl. He could hardly keep from fainting away.

### 155

When the count had slain his first son and let his blood run into the precious bowl, he laid the head beside its neck and stepped over to the other child. He lifted the steel sword and brought it down on the neck, collected the blood in the gleaming bowl of pure gold and then put the head back. The count covered the two boys with a rare and costly carpet and hurried out of the room, bolting the door behind him.

Amile went back to count Ami, who lay leprous in his bed.

### 156

Amile came back to count Ami, who lay leprous in his vaulted room. He was holding the bowl brimming with the blood of his two beheaded sons.

Ami saw him and was beside himself with horror. He cried out: "My God, why was I ever brought into this world!"

### 157

You can imagine how Ami shuddered when he saw the blood in
the shining bowl. But noble Amile called to his friend: "Good
lord Ami, now you can rise! If such an act can heal your body
and God of glory is ready to restore your health, then, by my
faith in Saint Omer, I do not regret the death of my two sons."

Ami got up and began to weep. Now he had proof that his
friend would stop at nothing to bring about his cure. Amile
fetched a large tub for his companion, but Ami was so weak that
he almost found it too hard to step in.

### 158

Ami was now in the tub; count Amile was holding the round
bowl. With the red blood, he washed his friend's forehead, his
eyes and his mouth, his arms, his legs, his belly, his whole body,
his feet and thighs and hands and shoulders. He bathed him all
over in blood.

### 159

Amile was worthy and noble. He washed with the blood the
mouth and the face of his companion. Ami could well believe
the count to be his friend, since he had slain for him his only two
sons.

Now listen, lords, to the miracle worked by Jesus Christ. As soon as the blood touched the leper's forehead, the scaly crust that covered him began to fall; his hands grew smooth, his belly and his chest. When his friend Amile saw this, he gave thanks to God the King and all the saints in heaven.

### 160

Count Amile was jubilant to see his friend healed and healthy. He saw once more Ami's white hands, and you can be sure both men were overjoyed. "God," they said, "sovereign Father, thanks be to You and all Your saints, good heavenly Father!"

### 161

Once Ami was cured and well, Amile, I tell you, was full of gladness. He embraced and kissed Ami, and offered thanks and praises to glorious God.

Count Amile, who was a gracious man, then hurried to his room and chose fine garments: two matching sets that pleased him, coats and surcoats and well-tailored cloaks trimmed in rich brocade. Ami, who was now healthy and well, put on these clothes, and so did Amile.

No man who saw the two counts so dressed, and this is the honest truth, could have told them apart; they were the very image of each other.

### 162

The barons were both wearing fine robes. They had the same face, the same nose and chin, the same gestures and speech; they looked so much alike that no man could tell which count was Ami and which one Amile.

Once they were dressed, they left for Saint Simon's, a church of great fame. Belissant had gone there, too, for her prayers, and there was a great crowd at mass. Now noble Ami and Amile started down the steps of the palace.

### 163

Hand in hand, they went down the steps of the palace. Steadfast and strong, the two barons strode down from the palace to level ground. Either one might have been the lord of the castle. Townsmen and peasants stared at them in wonder, for they did not know and could not tell which of the pair was their lord; everyone was uncertain.

### 164

The people were whispering about the two barons, unable to tell them apart or say to which one they owed their allegiance: it was as if the two counts had been a single man.

The companions made no pause till they reached the church where the beautiful and graceful Belissant was at prayer. Hand in hand, they went in and crossed themselves just as mass ended and the people were leaving. Amile's wife, too, was coming out; but when she came face to face with the counts, she was stunned by the wonder of their sameness and fell to the ground in a faint.

A hundred people or more ran up and, when she revived, they could all hear her say: "My lords, by our Savior, I know for certain that one of you is Amile the brave warrior and my husband, but I cannot say which of you is he." Amile said: "I am your husband, Belissant, and this is the valiant Ami, who suffered so long as a leper; but Jesus Christ has saved him and now, as you see, he is healed."

At that, the lady stretched her arms up toward God, and two thousand onlookers gave their thanks to the almighty King. The bells rang out, and priests and clerks sang forth praises, and a hundred people or more burst into tears of joy.

Amile said: "Stop this rejoicing and let us cry out in mourning instead, for my sons are slain and dead. I killed them with my own steel sword; I struck off their heads and let the blood run into a silver bowl, then bathed Ami with it, and he was cured of his sickness at once. But it was done at the urging of our Father Jesus Christ, who is the source of all good. Now, then, leave your rejoicing and you will see my torment and my martyrdom and my unending grief. Once we have buried my sons as befits them, strike off our heads right away! We have merited death."

## 165

Amile, the stalwart knight, continued: "Come away, my good people, guards, merchants, knights, scholars! Let us go up to the main hall of the castle, and there you will witness a harsher fate than you could ever have imagined."

Then you could have seen the people thronging up to the palace as the tolling of the bells in every church added to the mournful din.  You could have seen a procession of crosses and sweet-smelling censers and all those priests, in loud and grieving voices, chanting the hymn for the dead.

Belissant did not tarry, but hurried toward the room before anyone else, crying and weeping, tearing at her hair, bewailing her bitter loss.  She flung open the door.

What a miracle God worked at that moment!

Under the netting, she found her children sitting up in the bed and laughing.  The blessed boys were playing with an apple carved in gold.  The mother, amazed at the miraculous sight, fell senseless to the floor.

Even before she could come to herself, the wondrous room was filled and overflowed with people.  As Belissant threw her arms around her sons and kissed them, the news of God's miracle was fast being passed from person to person in the great crowd: clergy and scholars and everyone else learned that the children had been raised from the dead.

Amile heard, and so did stalwart Ami. I can't deny the two counts were overjoyed, for they loved the two boys.

### 166

When Belissant saw the children at play, she ran to clasp them in her arms.  If you had seen all those people hurrying into the room, all those soldiers and townspeople and young girls crowding in and crying joyous thanks to Jesus Christ, you would have seen a wonder to remember.

Count Ami could not push through the press, but heard the news that God had just raised his sons. Beautiful Belissant found her way back through the crowd, leading the beloved children along. She had had them dressed and made ready, those two whose beauty had no match even as far as Montcler, and led them into the main hall. When noble Amile saw them, he ran to kiss them and hug them; nor could Ami tire of embracing them.

The people all around looked on in awe. Belissant said: "Lord Amile, my good baron, if I had known this morning at dawn that you were going to sacrifice my children, I swear to you I would have stayed to help you collect their young blood." These words brought tears to countless eyes and moved all the people who heard them.

You can be sure there was no end of joy, and everyone started out for the church with the dearly-loved children. The bells pealed forth all by themselves, and the singers chanted loud and clear. What jubilation you could have seen in honor of that miracle!

### 167

There was much joy in the town of Riviers because Ami had been healed, but even greater joy because a miracle had brought the two beheaded boys back to life.

Amile's herald proclaimed through the city that no one should be so bold as to take his meal at home that day; everyone, townsman and stranger, poor or rich, was to come to court: there would be abundance and plenty for all. The people came as commanded, and no door was closed to them that day. Whoever wanted to eat was welcomed and had bread and wine, mead and claret and flesh of oxen, game and boar; whoever wanted to eat had his fill. When the meal was done and the drinking was over, servants and young men took down the tables; the court withdrew, and the hearty guests went on their way. The two counts were alone in the hall.

Ami had not forgotten his two good servants. On that day of his cure, he dubbed both of them knights, for they had endured great hardship and suffered great pains for their lord.

Now Ami said to Amile: "Dear friend, I think the time has come for me to see my wife."

## 168

"Good Amile," said worthy Ami, "it's true, I tell you, that I am eager to see Lubias with her smiling eyes and see my son Girard."

"Do not go," said his gracious companion; "I'll give you half of my holdings if you stay. But if you really want to leave, I shall go with you, and without a moment's delay."

That night they agreed to leave and they were to set out the next day.

## 169

Nothing further was said that night. The next day, when it grew light, they arose and had their gear made ready, their animals trussed and loaded. Count Amile went to take leave of his beloved wife, beautiful Belissant; he reminded her to watch over his domains with care and to safeguard the honor of their children, for it would be a while before his return.

I tell you, though, nothing will ever come of that thought: Amile will never see his lady again.

## 170

The two friends made haste; they had all their great gear harnessed and loaded, and set out from Riviers at midday.

They rode steadily down the great highway till they reached Blaye, and there they found lodgings with the innkeeper Gautier. He offered them rich and fitting comfort, and the two well-loved barons were pleased with their welcome.

Count Ami, God keep him from harm, wanted to wait awhile before going to the palace. He wanted to ask about Lubias, the woman he had wed, and learn what life she was leading, what good she was doing, what her prayers were for her husband's health; but, above all, he was eager to ask about his son Girard, whom he held so dear, and hear whether he surpassed other knights on the field.

At that point in his thoughts, his good host Gautier came in to call the two counts to their meal. He greeted them and said: "Come wash; everything is ready, and the tables are set."

## 171

At Gautier's inn, a fine supper was ready for the counts; their own squires set up the tables, and when they sat down after washing, they were served well and honored. The companions dined together and shared a single goblet.

Their host Gautier looked at them a long while and recognized his lord Ami; he chose his words like a man of good sense: "Barons," he said, "please don't be vexed by what I am going to say. I have looked at you both very closely; if the lord who once ruled this city had not been cast out as a leper, if he were as well now and as young as a long time ago when he married the sister of Hardret, I would say, in all truth, that one of you eating here side by side must be Ami of Blaye. Perhaps I am under some spell; yet I must say that one of you is Ami, our praiseworthy lord. He had a dear companion when he was still here in the castle, and there was no man alive who could tell them apart: they were the very image of each other."

172

Gautier went on: "As God is your protector, lord barons, don't keep it from me. I beseech you, by the Son of Mary, who suffered torment for us and was crucified and then came back to life on the third day, tell me your names, I beg you."

Ami boldly answered: "As God is my support, I am Ami; and this man, in truth, is Amile. I am freed of the sickness which brought me so much torment and made Lubias drive me outside the walls of this city and lock my son Girard in a cell, which was a wicked thing to do."

When he heard this, Gautier embraced him and kissed him, wetting Ami's face with his tears. He was beaming with joy.

## 173

There was much joy in the house on account of noble Ami. Gautier could hardly bring his embraces to an end. Ami asked about the son he held so dear, and his host said: "He has gone hunting. He rode by here this morning at daybreak, with no more than ten squires. He'll still be back tonight."

When they had eaten and the tables were removed, a messenger went through the streets bearing the news to all that Ami had returned healthy and well, and that he was at the inn of Gautier. He soon reached the palace and, without much ado, gave the news to Lubias. He told her that Ami was healthy and well, a handsome man with no match even as far as Montpellier. At this, Lubias was struck with wonder.

Meanwhile, you should have seen all those eager knights who had always held Ami so dear; you should have seen them leap onto their horses! They rushed off through the streets. Everyone followed, guards and squires, clerks and priests and princely lords. Everyone ran to Gautier's inn, and the whole house filled up with people. Everyone reached out to embrace Ami.

Just then, Girard, back from the hunt, rode into town through the rear gate, carrying his mountain falcon on his wrist. When he saw the people running and rushing about, and all those banners waving in the streets, he thought that fierce Charlemagne had come to assault his city.

But a squire came up and said: "My lord, Jesus Christ be praised for the news I bring you! Your father, whom you loved so much, has come back healed and healthy and well." When Girard heard that, he fell back in a faint and, if not for the stirrups, would have fallen from his horse. His men saw and ran to revive him, weeping with wonder and joy.

## 174

When Girard heard that his father was well, he gave thanks to the Lord. Then he called to the messenger and said: "Friend, good brother, take me, in God's name, to the house where he is." And straight to the inn the two of them went, with no stop or delay.

Worthy Girard jumped down from his horse and went into the house. He pushed his way through the crowd, hurrying to kiss and embrace his father. Ami clasped him in turn and could not let go. No one could describe all the joy that the son gave to his father.

## 175

At Gautier's inn, filled with jubilation, father and son never wearied of embracing each other.

As for Lubias, she dressed and put on her finest jewels. When she was ready, she went down from the palace and made straight for the inn.

Count Ami, as handsome now as he had ever been, was out in the garden. Lubias wasted no time; she arrived and, surrounded by onlookers, hurried up to Ami and took him by the hand. "Friend, good brother," she said, "I offer myself to you; I am yours to do with as you will."

"Move away," said the count brusquely; "you can never be my wife again. You heaped shame on me when you cast me out of my city and drove me into grief and hardship, and with your witch's spell made everyone believe I was a stinking cripple...

You gave me a little hovel right outside the walls: well, it still stands, and a fine reward awaits you there! That's where you will now be put to live in misery. For food, you will have no more than a scant quarter loaf a day, or even less than that. Knights and guards! take her away, take her away as fast as you can—and bind her hands tight." And that is what the count's men did when they heard his order.

A crowd of people followed as they led Lubias away and made straight for the hut. There the lady was left and the escort went back to the city.

She had been in the hovel a week, when count Ami felt overcome with pity; he fetched her back and restored her to her domain. Count Ami, so handsome and healthy, now dubbed his son Girard a knight and gave all his holdings into his hands; to his two serfs he gave a large estate.

Powerful count Ami took up the cross, and his companion hastened to do so as well. Count Amile sent word to Belissant that she should watch over his domains and remember to honor his two sons, for they would never again see him in their lifetime.

Then the barons wasted no time; the next day at dawn, they started on their way from Blaye to Jerusalem and the Holy Sepulcher.

## 176

In the morning, the two counts rode out of Blaye to seek God's pardon beyond the sea. Many valiant knights gave them an escort, together with Girard, the young baron of great fame. They wept sad tears at their parting, and Girard kissed his father on the chin; then the escort turned back to the castle at Blaye.

The two counts pressed forward with God's blessing. They

rode steadily ahead and unhindered, till they reached a port on the sea. The winds were good, and they crossed without oars. They went straight to the Holy Sepulcher and fervently kissed the True Cross where Jesus Christ our Lord suffered his passion.

Then the good barons returned and sailed back untroubled across the sea. On their Aragonese steeds, the two barons rode safely through Provence together.

## 177

When the counts had crossed the sea, they traveled through Lombardy on their way back home. They took their way through Mortara, and there good destiny brought them to their end.

There they passed away, as we all have heard. Pilgrims on the road well know the tomb where they lie buried.

Here ends the song I have sung of the good and worthy barons Ami and Amile, who gained such fame that they will be remembered till the end of time.

\* \* \*

## NOTES

### LAISSE 1

*Santiago de Compostela:* City in Galicia, in northwest Spain, which was one of the major shrines of pilgrimage in the Middle Ages.

*Mortara:* Town in northern Italy, between Turin and Pavia, situated along the French pilgrimage route to Rome.

### LAISSE 2

*Berry:* County, later duchy, of central France, whose capital was Bourges.

*Auvergne:* Interior province of south-central France, whose capital was Clermont-Ferrand.

### LAISSE 3

*Bourges:* Capital of the old province of Berry, in central France.

### LAISSE 4

*Nevers:* Capital of the old province of Nivernais (duchy of Burgundy), in central France, about 50 km. east of Bourges.

*Abbey of Vézelay:* Romanesque abbey near Avallon in central France, about 75 km. northeast of Nevers. Saint Bernard preached the Second Crusade there in 1147.

*Burgundy:* Former duchy in east-central France.

*Monjeu:* The Great Saint Bernard Pass in the Alps, between Switzerland and the Italian Aosta Valley.

*Chomin:* Locality apparently between Mortara and Pavia; precise identification uncertain.

*Chastel:*   Locality apparently near Pavia; precise identification uncertain.

*Pavia:*   Capital of medieval Lombardy, in north-central Italy.


LAISSE 5

*Clermont:*   Clermont-Ferrand, capital of Auvergne, in south-central France.

*Traves:*   Town in Italy (?).

*Mount Chevrol:*   This might designate the Capitoline Hill, highest of the seven hills of Rome, but it is far more probably the town of Capriglia in Tuscany, northwest of Lucca, situated along one of the main routes taken by French travelers to Rome.

*Borgo:*   Town outside Rome, apparently near the Sant' Angelo bridge over the Tiber.

*Nero's Gardens:*   Name for the Vatican or Rome recalling the ancient Gardens of Agrippa and Circus of Nero.

*Apulia:*   Province of southeastern Italy.


LAISSE 6

*Garigliano:*   River in central Italy flowing into the Gulf of Gaeta north of Naples. (The name in the French text is Garrigant, which may designate instead Mount Gargano, which is on the promontory of northern Apulia that forms the "spur" of Italy.)

*Calabria:*   Province of southwestern Italy.

*Gascony:*   Former duchy of southwestern France.


LAISSE 7

*Siena:*   City in Tuscany, about 60 km. south of Florence.

*niello ring:* A relatively common type of ring produced by filling the channels of ornamentally engraved silver with a metallic substance black in color.

*silver mark:* Weight of silver roughly equivalent to eight ounces and worth approximately two-and-one-half times as much as the monetary pound, or *livre.*

## LAISSE 9

*besant:* Silver or gold coin originally minted in Byzantium, whence its name, and widely used in western Europe during the Middle Ages.

## LAISSE 11

*half a league:* Roughly two kilometers.

*golden spurs:* The same spurs were said to be of silver in laisse 9. This is one of numerous instances of factual inconsistency in our poem, partly due no doubt, as in the present case, to the exigencies of assonance and meter.

## LAISSE 14

*hauberks:* Garments of chain mail intended to protect the body from head to knee; also called coats of mail.

## LAISSE 15

*hundredweight of pennies:* An insignificant amount of money expressed, derisively, in terms of one of the smallest monetary divisions, a silver penny, or *denier,* being only one two-hundred-fortieth of a pound, or *livre.*

## LAISSE 17

*sat . . . on the marble floor:* Medieval castles tended to be only sparsely furnished; even if the poet wishes to enhance Charlemagne's dwelling by attributing a marble floor to it, he clearly sees no need to furnish it with chairs as well.

LAISSE 18
*Nivelles:* Town in Belgium, about 30 km. south of Brussels.

*olive tree:* Occurring, too, in laisses 19, 22, and 72, this is hardly a realistic detail. Its presence here may be attributed to a desire for poetic enhancement of the setting. Cf. M. Bloch, *Feudal Society,* trans. Manyon (Chicago, 1961), p. 97: "travelers. . .acquainted [the] northern poets with the beauty of the Mediterranean olive tree, which with a naive taste for the exotic and a fine contempt for local colour the chansons plant boldly on the hills of Burgundy or Picardy."

*one thousand pounds:* A considerable sum, the monetary pound, or *livre,* being roughly equivalent to 100 grams, or three ounces, of silver.

LAISSE 19
*Saint Lambert's:* Perhaps the cathedral of Liège in Belgium, the best-known church bearing this name.

*a thousand:* The evident contradiction between this figure and the four thousand mentioned two paragraphs above is one of the various indications of the epic poet's disdain of consistency in rendering realistic detail.

LAISSE 20
*prime:* The first of the seven canonical hours of the day, six a.m. or else sunrise.

LAISSE 23
*Joincherres:* Town near Paris, perhaps present-day Jonquières.

LAISSE 28
*Blaye:* Blaye-et-Sainte-Luce, port on the Gironde, not far from the southern Atlantic coast of France and near Bordeaux.

LAISSE 30
*apostle:* This word was commonly used in Old French to designate the pope.

LAISSE 31

*France:* Used in Old French to refer either to the Kingdom of France or to the Ile-de-France.

*a thousand:* This figure is in contradiction with the four hundred mentioned in laisse 30. For similar inconsistency, see laisse 19.

LAISSE 32

*Valsecrée:* This name ('secret valley') is given to a number of different places in Old French epic poetry, all of which are probably fictive.

LAISSE 34

*vixen under the tree:* A use of the Aesopian fable of the fox and the sour grapes which is rather striking in its shift of focus; Ami is assuring Amile that, if he simply keeps his distance, Belissant will not long find him attractive.

LAISSE 40

*a hundred sols:* Sum equivalent to five pounds, or *livres,* or 1200 pennies, or *deniers.* To gauge its generosity, see laisse 15 and note.

LAISSE 45

*Curse the man . . .:* This exclamation must be understood as expressing the response of the knights rather than the sentiment of the narrator.

LAISSE 46

*if he is harmed or hurt . . .:* With this statement Charlemagne accepts the Queen's terms and warns that Amile, now spoken for, is not to be harmed outside the lists.

LAISSE 53

*whom I left so sick:* Ami, thanks to his dream (laisse 49), knows whom he is about to meet and, with this excuse of Lubias' sickness, is inventing a pretext that will allow Amile, impersonating him, to turn back to Blaye with Ami's men. Amile, in laisse 61, will reinforce this argument by alleging that he himself is not feeling well; he will make further use of this fabrication in laisse 66.

*Montpellier:* Major city in the south, a few miles from the Mediterranean, west of the Rhône.

## LAISSE 62
*Arabian steeds:* Arabian horses, whether from the Near East or from Spain, were particularly prized in medieval France.

## LAISSE 64
*sword:* A sword placed in bed between a man and a woman was a traditional sign of the chastity of their relations.

## LAISSE 66
*Only the other day:* Chronological realism is clearly not one of the poet's main concerns. It is indeed hard to reconcile the speaker's presence at Laon "the other day" with the relative brevity of Ami's journey from Blaye only halfway up to Paris and his (really Amile's) almost immediate return.

*Laon:* City about 130 km. northeast of Paris, one of the most stable strongholds of the Carolingian dynasty and site of one of the first Gothic cathedrals.

*Besançon:* Capital of the old province of Franche-Comté, in east-central France, about 50 km. from Switzerland.

*The other day:* Lubias is fabricating a visit by Amile to Blaye during Ami's brief absence (laisses 51-62).

*Rogation Days:* The three days before Ascension Thursday, set aside for solemn processions to invoke divine mercy.

## LAISSE 69
*Holy Innocents:* The children of Bethlehem slaughtered at Herod's order following the birth of Jesus; see Matthew 2:16.

*Longinus:* The soldier who pierced Christ with his spear; see John

19:34. According to medieval tradition, blood spurting from the wound healed him of an ophthalmic disease and led to his conversion.

*Nicodemus:* Prominent Pharisee, sympathetic to Jesus, who assisted in the burial; see John 3:1-21, 7:50-51, 19:39-42.

LAISSE 70
*Saint Victor's:* Abbey of Saint Victor, founded in the twelfth century on the left bank of the Seine just outside Paris; the site is now within the city.

LAISSE 73
*Saint Denis:* First bishop of Paris (third century), whose relics, from the early seventh century on, were enshrined at the basilica of his name, just north of Paris.

*Saint Martin:* Bishop of Tours (fourth century), who became perhaps the most popular saint of medieval France.

*Pepin:* Pepin the Short (714-768), son of Charles Martel, founder of the Carolingian dynasty, father of Charlemagne.

LAISSE 79
*Pavian helmet:* Pavia was important, at the time of our poem, in the production of arms and armor. Later in the thirteenth century, the center of the Lombard industry shifted to Milan.

*Pavia and . . . Piedmont:* Pavia is actually in Lombardy, south of Milan, and not, as the poem suggests, in the neighboring region of the Piedmont.

LAISSE 80
*Moorish hauberk:* Like Lombardy, Islamic Spain was important and prestigious in the production of arms and armor.

*Aragonese mule:* Spanish mounts were among those particularly prized in medieval France.

LAISSE 84

*Gascon charger:* Gascony, in the southwest, was the region of medieval France most renowned for its horses.

LAISSE 87

*Riviers:* Generally considered a city of the poet's invention, this may in fact refer to the old port of Rivière-Saint-Sauveur, near present-day Honfleur, at the mouth of the Seine.

*Dunne:* This is presented by the poet here and again in laisse 102 as a river; as such it has no reality. The true reference, apparently unknown to our poet but not to his predecessor(s), may be to the dune-lined coast near Rivière-Saint-Sauveur, an area formerly known, precisely, as Dune or Dunes.

LAISSE 91

*with the consent of . . . Ami:* It was characteristic of companionage that the marriage of one man should require the consent of the other.

LAISSE 94

*Touraine:* Inland region of west-central France.

*Poitiers:* Capital of the old province of Poitou, south of Touraine, in west-central France.

*Saint-Jean-d'Angély:* Town about 100 km. southwest of Poitiers, about 90 km. north of Blaye.

*Bordeaux:* Major river-port about 30 km. south of Blaye.

LAISSE 96

*quartered shield:* A shield divided into two upper and two lower fields for the display of four coats of arms.

LAISSE 99

*vielles:* The vielle, or hurdy-gurdy, was a stringed instrument in the general shape of a lute, played both by keys and by a rotating wheel controlled by a crank.

LAISSE 102

*dromonds:* Large, speedy war-vessels with one or more banks of oars.


LAISSE 117

*church of Saint Michael:* There is no record of such a church outside the old walls of Blaye; occurring at the end of a line in the original text, the name was probably chosen for assonance.


LAISSE 121

*Saint Gilles:* Apparently the town of Saint-Gilles-du-Gard, near Nîmes and Arles, at the edge of the Rhône delta. Its famous church was built around 1200, roughly the time of our poem.


LAISSE 123

*Montramble:* Unidentified locality between Blaye and the Great Saint Bernard Pass (Monjeu); or else, a corruption of Pontramble, for Italian Pontremoli, a town between Parma and La Spezia along the traditional French route to Rome. In the latter case, laisse 123 ends with a considerable telescoping of the journey, and laisse 124 must be regarded as recapitulative rather than simply sequential.


LAISSE 125

*Monbardon:* This is in all likelihood Monte Bardone, the Appenine pass today called La Cisa, located about 15 km. north of Pontremoli; see note on Montramble (laisse 123).

*Monjoie:* The Mount of Joy, or Mons Gaudii, today Mount Mario, situated on the right bank of the Tiber a few kilometers north of the Vatican.


LAISSE 127

*two brothers:* An instance of inconsistency in detail; laisse 3 mentions four brothers, and laisse 133 mentions three.


LAISSE 131

*sixty sols:* See note to laisse 40.

LAISSE 133
   *three . . . brothers:* See note to laisse 127.


LAISSE 135
   *Brittany:* Region of northwest France forming the peninsula between the English Channel and the Bay of Biscay.

   *Mont-Saint-Michel:* Rocky island just off the coast approximately at the point where Brittany and Normandy meet, accessible by land at low tide; a well-known pilgrims' shrine even before the construction (1203-28) of the great Gothic abbey.

   *one hundred silver marks:* See note on silver mark, laisse 7.


LAISSE 136
   *two weeks:* If Riviers is indeed to be identified with Rivière-Saint-Sauveur (see note to laisse 87), sea travel from Mont-Saint-Michel would have required circumnavigating the peninsula of Cotentin as well as sailing along the coast of present-day Calvados and might in fact have taken two weeks.

   *rattle:* Lepers were usually required to warn the healthy of their approach by means of a rattle, a bell, a small horn or the like.


LAISSE 138
   *Saint-Michel:* Market-town outside of Riviers, probably of the poet's invention; at the end of a line in the original text, the name may have been chosen for the sake of assonance.


LAISSE 140
   *African silk:* The most prestigious varieties of this luxury fabric were imported from the Islamic world.


LAISSE 145
   *Saint Simon's:* This is apparently a fictive church, its name chosen for the sake of assonance.

LAISSE 148

*for all the gold in Russia:* A formulaic phrase occurring with a wide range of place-names; Russia, in this instance, not only connotes great abundance, but also, occurring at the end of a line, fits into the assonance pattern of the laisse.

LAISSE 151

*Duurstede:* Wijk te Duurstede in the Netherlands, an important port of the Rhine delta in the Middle Ages. The phrase 'as far as Duresté' occurs formulaically in a number of Old French epics.

LAISSE 154

*silver bowl:* Consistency in factual detail is superseded by the requirements of assonance: the same bowl is made of gold in laisses 151 and 155, and again of silver in laisse 164.

LAISSE 157

*Saint Omer:* This reference might be taken as corroborating the identification of Riviers with Rivière-Saint-Sauveur (see note to laisse 87), for Saint Omer is the same Audemarus for whom the neighboring town of Pont-Audemer is named.

LAISSE 166

*Montcler:* There is no satisfactory identification of this place-name, which, in any event, has no narrative importance but simply serves to evoke a great distance.

LAISSE 167

*took down the tables:* Commonly consisting of separable trestles and top boards, tables were often assembled only for meals and removed afterwards; cf. laisses 171 and 173.

LAISSE 171

*sister:* An instance of inconsistency in detail; in laisse 28, Lubias is identified as Hardret's niece.

LAISSE 173

*mountain falcon on his wrist:*  A practitioner of the noble sport of hunting with a falcon would normally carry the bird perched on his wrist.

LAISSE 176

*Provence:*  The great region of southeastern France bordering on the Mediterranean.  This detail of the knights' itinerary is inconsistent with their death at Mortara and, even more strikingly, with the statement in laisse 177 that "they traveled through Lombardy on their way home."

LAISSE 177

*Pilgrims on the road:*  This phrase should not be understood as implying that the knights' tomb was a destination of pilgrims; it was simply located along the route—the Via Francigena, other points of which were mentioned earlier—that was followed by most French pilgrims and other travelers to Rome.